The Impulse of Freedom in Islam

The Impulse of Freedom in Islam

John van Schaik
Christine Gruwez
& Cilia ter Horst

FOREWORD BY Abdulwahid van Bommel
AFTERWORD BY Ibrahim Abouleish

Lindisfarne Books | 2014

2014
LINDISFARNE BOOKS
An imprint of Anthroposophic Press / SteinerBooks
610 Main St., Great Barrington, MA 01230
www.steinerbooks.org

Copyright © 2014 by John van Schaik, Christine Gruwez, and Cilia ter Horst. All rights reserved. No part of this publication may be reproduced, stored in a retrieval system, or transmitted, in any form or by any means, electronic, mechanical, photocopying, recording, or otherwise, without the prior written permission of the publisher.

Translated by Philip Mees
Translator's note: The quotations from the Koran are taken from
http://quod.lib.umich.edu/k/koran/

Cover image copyright © Pikoso.kz (shutterstock.com)
Cover and book design: Jeanne DePrince Bowen

LIBRARY OF CONGRESS CONTROL NUMBER: 2014931997

Print ISBN: 978-1-58420-163-2
eBook ISBN: 978-1-58420-164-9

Contents

Foreword *Abdulwahid van Bommel* 7
Introduction *John van Schaik* 13

PART 1 Islam in Historical and Theological Perspective
John van Schaik 17

   1. Post-Colonial Image of Islam 19
   2. History of Islam 35
   3. Allah: Predestination or Freedom? 45
   4. Jesus in Islam 65

PART 2 The Freedom Impulse of Mohammed Abduh and Rudolf Steiner
Cilia ter Horst 79

   5. Background: Types of Freedom in Mohammed Abduh's Life 81
   6. Between God and Nature: The Free Will of the Human Being According to Rudolf Steiner and Mohammed Abduh 89

PART 3 The Philosophy of Freedom in Iranian Islam
Christine Gruwez 107

   7. Thinking in the Light of the Spirit: Elements from Iranian Philosophy 109

PART 4 Rudolf Steiner on Islam
John van Schaik 157

Afterword: Freedom in Islam *Ibrahim Abouleish* 175
Notes 179

Foreword

Abdulwahid van Bommel

No religion without freedom of religion.

During the last decade of the twentieth and the first decade of the twenty-first centuries, religion has begun to occupy a negative or, at least, a controversial place in the thinking of many people, especially in Europe. In this regard, Islam is the clear champion in its ability to attract negative attention. The bastion of the right-minded center, in which there are still groups of balanced people who understand that it is just as absurd to say that Al-Qaeda and the Taliban are representative of Islam as to say that the Spanish Inquisition, apartheid, Auschwitz, Hiroshima or Abu Graib are representative of Christianity—this category of balanced people is beginning to disappear.

The fact that human rights are formulated as human freedoms, and that Islam is rather perceived as robbing people of freedom, plays a central role in the controversy. "All the freedom we have won in this part of the world is in danger of being dismantled by Islam," seems to be a rather premature suggestion. It is therefore important to give our attention to the thoughts about freedom in the basic texts of Islam and in Muslim history, not as naïve assertions against the severe tide of salafistic* legal and opportunistic Arabic scholars, but rather as the basis for the development of an Islamic theology for the future of our children and grandchildren.

Many Muslim thinkers have given attention to the concept of freedom (*hurriyya*), freedom of choice (*ikhtiyar*) and free will (*irada*). Lawyers place these concepts in the perspective of legal terminology, of the use and abuse of freedom; Sufis strive for inner freedom by freeing themselves of the fetters of the lower

---

* Translator's note: A *Salafi* is a Muslim who emphasizes the *Salaf* ("predecessors" or "ancestors"), the earliest Muslims, as model examples of Islamic practice. (Source: Wikipedia)

self; theologians are primarily interested in the relationship between human and divine will and in the way the latter restricts the former in its freedom; and philosophers take human free will as the basis of their way of thinking. The debate about whether God restricts or determines human free will can in a certain sense be viewed as a precursor of today's discussions about the relationship between innate and acquired characteristics.

We can see the consequences of the fact that Allah created all his creations in certain relationships and proportions[1] in the specific qualities and characteristics of all living things. Everything has a specific time and place; this time comes to an end with death.[2] The manner in which the human being uses his free will determines his destination both in this life and in the hereafter. The discussions that arose on this subject in the first centuries of Islam were for the time being closed by Hasan al-Basri (died 728), the leader of the Qadarites, by his statement: "Moral action implies freedom. Divine guidance comes from Allah, error from the human being."

Fatalists deny the human free will. This means that human responsibility is a senseless concept. If we are forced into our actions, the basis for all ethics is pulled out from under our feet; then all law and all legal systems in this world cease to have any meaning. Human will is able to deviate from divine will, and can even go against it; in religion this is called sin. Also for Islamic law a person must have acted out of free will. If someone acts under compulsion, ignorance or insanity, he is not responsible.

Muslim philosophers are not only interested in the dialectic relationship between human freedom and responsibility but also in the relationship between divine power and this freedom. Through the centuries the standard question has been: "If human life is determined by divine decree, how can the human being then be responsible for his actions?" Then the following verses from the Koran become incomprehensible: "surely Allah does not change the condition of a people until they change their own condition"[3] and "that man shall have nothing but what he strives for."[4] The human being is free to choose for God's guidance or to reject it, and he is responsible for that choice. "Every human child is born with the inclination toward the good," says the prophet Mohammed. The fact that the human being is born in a state of *fitra** is confirmed in the following verse from

---

* Translator's note: *Fitra* means the human constitution. According to Islamic theology, human beings are born with an innate inclination of *tawhid* (Oneness), which is encapsulated in the *fitra* along with compassion, intelligence, *ihsan* (perfection, excellence) and all other attributes that embody what it is to be human. (Source: Wikipedia)

the Koran: "Then set your face upright for religion in the right state—the nature made by Allah in which He has made men."[5]

In spite of the differences of opinion between black-and-white thinkers and more differentiating ones, there are countless readers who find the Koran an inspiring and inspired book. They love its text as it was before it fell into the hands of the scholars of religion, law and Arabism. They also love the elements of freedom as these appear in the Koran for uncorrupted readers. Here I am highlighting a few of those passages.

"There is no compulsion in religion,"[6] neither to begin believing and embrace a religion, nor to prevent people from leaving that religion or to abjure the faith. This freedom is the very core of every faith. Without this core of freedom faith has absolutely no value. Freedom of religion is a God-given right and human beings can only confirm it.

In the Koran we see the moment when God taught Adam the "names of things" and then asked the angels to name the things. They responded that outside of God they had no knowledge, and Adam shared his knowledge of the names with them. Thereupon God commanded the angels to prostrate themselves before Adam. All did so, except Iblis[7] who refused out of hubris and declared that he was better than Adam: "I am better than he: You created me from fire, and him from clay."[8] The matter is clear: Iblis does not obey God's command to kneel for Adam. Here we have to note that in Islam a difference is made between God's command and His will. The whole idea of the command is that one can follow it or ignore it. Free will enables us to attain to great heights, or to fall into great depths, on the basis of our choices and decisions.

While it is true that God expelled Iblis from paradise, as soon as the latter had been cast off he immediately started pleading with God for favors.[9] "My Lord! because Thou hast made life evil to me, I will certainly make (evil) fair-seeming to them on earth, and I will certainly cause them all to deviate.[10]... Then I will certainly come to them from before them and from behind them, and from their right-hand side and from their left-hand side; and Thou shalt not find most of them thankful."[11] This remarkable first act of the human drama and the powers of good and evil shows that in this elementary area there exists the greatest possible freedom. Iblis had the freedom to obey God's command or not. He did not, and then continued to negotiate with the Creator.

The Koran describes the primordial moment when God asks the human souls: "Am I not your Lord? They said: Yes! we bear witness!"[12] Exactly on this point, the first human couple undergoes a test practically immediately. "And We said: O Adam! Dwell you and your wife in the garden and eat from it a plenteous (food) wherever you wish and do not approach this tree, for then you will be of the unjust."[13] "But the Shaitan made an evil suggestion to him; he said: 'O Adam! Shall I guide you to the tree of immortality and a kingdom which decays not?'"[14] The tree may be a metaphor for the boundaries the human being must set for himself so as not to act against his own nature. The temptation exists to look for the eternal here on earth and to deny the hereafter. Adam and Eve together transgressed against God's prohibition; in doing so they gave the first demonstration in human history of the exercise of the free will. The similarities between the rebellion of Iblis and that of Adam are striking. Both are witness to the fact that the value of faith is determined by the freedom to confess that faith and obey or disobey Allah's commands. That is the side of the human being. The Koran explains the meaning of existence in part as the ability to pass the test of existence. Every test and every exam has significance only if the one who is tested has the freedom to make choices.[15] According to the Koran this freedom goes so far that one can choose to believe or not to believe: "And say: The truth is from your Lord, so let him who please believe, and let him who please disbelieve."[16]

Islam views religious diversity as something natural that is connected with the free will and, therefore, with the capacity of the human being to make choices. God could have imposed on all human beings to follow one truth like a law of nature, but He did not do this: "... If Allah had pleased He would have made you (all) a single people, but that He might try you in what He gave you."[17] The Koran also says: "And if your Lord had pleased, surely all those who are in the earth would have believed, all of them; will you then force men till they become believers?"[18]

If God in His all-encompassing wisdom did not compel humanity to follow one principle, should we human beings then do this among each other?

In his farewell speech Mohammed called on all of humanity with the following words: "O people! Know that your Lord is one! You are all from Adam, and Adam is from dust." On other occasions he said: "He who shows no mercy to others shall receive no mercy from Allah. He among you who has minorities for enemies shall have me for enemy. Each one who oppresses a person of different faith [Jew or Christian] and imposes excessive burdens on him, shall face me as his accuser."[19]

According to the Koran every human being who lives according to a revelation, irrespective of the name of his faith, can reach heaven: "Surely those who believe, and those who are Jews, and the Christians, and the Sabians, whoever believes in Allah and the Last day and does good, they shall have their reward from their Lord, and there is no fear for them, nor shall they grieve."[20]

In the exceptionally sensitive area of belief or unbelief people are not permitted to make judgments on each other. Muslims too are not permitted to do this, neither among each other nor vis-à-vis others. The only one entitled to judge is God Himself: "Is not Allah the wisest of judges?"[21] Early in its revelation the Koran says already: "To you be your Way, and to me mine."[22] Even the prophet Mohammed does not have the task to judge: "Therefore do remind, for you are only a reminder. You are not a watcher over them."[23] "Therefore whoever goes aright, he goes aright for his own soul, and whoever goes astray, then say: I am only one of the warners."[24]

During fourteen centuries of Islam, all theology and doctrine for the practice of the faith has been formulated anew on the basis of selected texts to which one either attributed canonical value or not. It is quite possible to develop a theology of the future, in which the subject of freedom of religion forms an elementary part of the doctrine. Muslims should emphasize the universal values of Islam so that it can be recognized by a non-Muslim environment. We can begin to build the foundations of a theology of the future on the basis of values such as:

karama al-fard—the inviolability of each individual
hurriyya al-fard—the freedom of each individual
'adala idjtima'iyya—social justice
wa tasawi—and equality.

These values are summarized in the Koran text *Laqad Karamna bani Adam*: "We have honored the sons of Adam."[25]

May this book be a contribution to such a future.

Introduction

John van Schaik

Sometimes people ask me: "What is this about you and Islam?" My answer is then: "I am a Muslim, but not an Islamite." Total bewilderment. I explain that one can surrender to God (which is the meaning of the word Muslim) along the path of Islam, Christianity, Judaism, Buddhism, and so on, for all these religions confess belief in one (supreme) God. My path is that of Christianity, more specifically, of esoteric Christianity, especially as embodied in Anthroposophy. It is the purpose of the authors of this book to make a contribution to the image of Islam in the West out of their anthroposophical inspiration. That is one aspect of the book.

The other aspect comes from the scientific expertise of the authors in regard to Islam. The combination of anthroposophical inspiration and scientific expertise creates a third aspect, namely the originality with which the authors observe and view the problem of "Islam in the West."

It is specifically one aspect of Islam on which the authors wish to shine a light; this is the "freedom impulse of Islam." Freedom in Islam! For sure! In any case no less than in Christianity or any "ism." For freedom depends not on a religion, but on the way people practice their religion. Just like with the Christian Bible, so also with the Koran you can justify almost anything you want. And in the Koran you can find passages that defend the free will. See for instance Sura 76: 28-31. Islam is no more intolerant than Christianity or Buddhism. It is people who are intolerant.

And yet, it cannot be denied that there are many intolerant and fundamentalist Muslims. Neither can it be denied that there are many intolerant and fundamentalist Christians and Buddhists.

THE IMPULSE OF FREEDOM IN ISLAM

Every religion can be viewed at three levels:

1. The level of rituals, customs and tradition; this makes a religion a system of beliefs;
2. The level of theology;
3. The spiritual and mystical level.

At the level of rituals and tradition one can have respect for each other's customs and habits: "O, is that the way you do it!" At the level of theology we are dealing with questions of faith, and the demon of intolerance soon raises its head. And at the third level, we come to the core of every religion. This core is the fact that there is one God who is the same for all religions, beyond all rituals, customs and theology.

When these three levels are confused or comingled, we run into problems. Then this one God (level 3) becomes the one and only true God of your religion (level 2). And if this God then begins to prescribe (level 1) how you have to behave, the conditions for intolerance and unfreedom have been created. Then you get fundamentalism, whether it is Islamic, Christian or Buddhist fundamentalism. And then it is a small step to the use of force and violence in order to defend and spread your religion, whether it is the case of 9/11 or of "in God we trust" of the United States in Afghanistan.

The authors of this book are focused on the third, the mystical or spiritual level. It is the level of the intention or impulse of a religion, the level where the religion wants to reconnect with God.* Since intentions and impulses come from human beings—not from religions—this implies that, in our view, the basis of every religion is freedom. This freedom can be discovered at the level of spirituality and intention in every religion. We consider it necessary to highlight the freedom impulse of Islam because freedom in Islam is hardly ever mentioned in western discussions of Islam. We want to contribute to forging a "missing link."

Also in the work of Rudolf Steiner (1861-1925), the founder of Anthroposophy, it is not always clear at which of our three levels he is speaking about Islam. Sometimes he says something about "common" traditional Islam (level 1). Sometimes he makes theological comments (level 2). Here Steiner usually shows himself as a person of his time, of the western colonialism of the nineteenth century. Then Steiner emphasizes

---

* Translator's note: *Religion* is derived from the Latin *religare*, to connect.

INTRODUCTION

the fatalistic nature of what he called "Mohammedanism." This was a common view of the Orient in colonial Europe. These are not noteworthy comments. Steiner is relevant for the freedom impulse of Islam when he says things of a unique nature. This is the case in some of his comments on the impulse of Mohammed and Islam. He speaks at the third level when he says, among other things, that the original impulse of Mohammed most certainly includes a freedom impulse.

At the same time, Rudolf Steiner also makes rather severe comments on the fatalistic nature of Islam, but that is the Islam of his own time, not the Islam of the seventh to tenth centuries. In other words, the original freedom impulse of Islam has been snowed under in the course of history and tradition (level 1). We might well wonder whether Mohammed would still recognize Islam as it is today, just as we might wonder whether Jesus would recognize his freedom impulse in Christianity today, or Buddha in today's Buddhism.

In this book the authors are looking for the places where the freedom impulse of Islam is (still) working. Why are three western-Christian authors doing this? Because they are less impeded by all the "silt" that became deposited in the river of Islam in the course of time. However, this might also result in a certain one-sidedness. For this reason, we have included a brief contribution on the freedom impulse in Islam by the Egyptian Ibrahim Abouleish, as well as a foreword by the Dutch imam Abdulwahid van Bommel.

Part 1

Islam in Historical and Theological Perspective

John van Schaik

John van Schaik is a scholar of the history of religion. His contribution has, therefore, an historical aspect (chapters 1 and 2) and a religious-scientific one (chapters 3 and 4).

In the first chapter, he contends that the current western view of Islam continues to be determined by the image of Islam that arose in the middle of the nineteenth century, the time in which "superior" Europe colonized the world around it. Europe justified this imperialism on the basis of the idea of a "mandate for civilization." It was Europe's task, as seen by Europeans, to civilize the world.

The second chapter contains a brief review of the history of Islam. Long before the Islamic-Arabian conquests after 622, there had been Arabian migrations to the West. For instance, Arabian tribes had been living in Syria for centuries when the conquests started. And the other way around, Christianity had been known on the Arabian peninsula for centuries—some of Mohammed's relatives were Christians.

In chapter 3, the author considers the critical question of God's omnipotence versus human free will. Is Allah really an omnipotent God who excludes the free human will, the way it is often represented in the West? Things are more subtle than that. Moreover, Christianity also knows the conflict between predestination and free will. What is the real nature of this conflict in the Koran?

In Islam, Isa (Jesus) plays a very important role (chapter 4). In the Koran, Isa is called "the word" and "the spirit" of Allah. It is Isa who appears at the end of time to defeat the Antichrist. This is a reason to compare the image of Jesus in Islam with the Christological discussions in the seventh century—and today!

Chapter 1

Post-Colonial Image of Islam

In the opinion of the Palestinian professor Edward Wadie Said, the western image of Islam is largely determined by the colonial views of Islam at the end of the nineteenth century. Modern western Islamology came into being in the wake of colonialism. At the end of the nineteenth century, esotericists also arrived at an image that continues to influence current ideas about Islam, even today. The roots of our image of Islam, therefore, are lying in the period between 1850 and 1900. How did people at that time view Islam? In this chapter, the emphasis is on Germany, so that we can study the comments of Rudolf Steiner in their context.

Popular Discussion

The popular views of Islam in Europe around 1900 were determined by the distinction between *Occident* and *Orient*. Europe was the Occident and stood for Christian, rational, enlightened, humanistic, scientific and masculine. The Orient geographically encompassed everything east of the Bosporus (Istanbul). It was in everything the opposite of the European characteristics: not Christian, mysterious, exotic, dreamy, full of imagination and feminine. The picture of the exotic, dreamy East comes through, for instance, in the *Fairy Tales of a Thousand and One Nights*, which was translated into German between 1825 and 1838 by the Arabic scholar Max Habicht (1775-1839). At that time there were already French and English translations. Later in the nineteenth century appeared a new English translation by William Lane (1801-1876), who had lived for years among Muslims in Cairo under the name of Mansur Effendi. He was the author of many scientific publications about Islam and the Koran and was a member of the *Deutsche Morgenländische Gesellschaft* (German Oriental Society).

The West-East concept based on geography—and especially the concept of European superiority—is very old. We find it already in the fifth century BCE during the wars between the Greeks and the Persians, and even in the twentieth century CE it continues to be standard, says Edward Wadie Said (1935-2003) in his book *Orientalism*.[26] Said was born in Palestine and taught comparative literature at Columbia University, New York. In his book he developed the so-called "post-colonial theory" which says that, although there are no longer any colonies, the world is continuing to think and act according to the concept West–enlightened versus East–decadent. Evidently this scheme is part of the collective archetypal subconscious of the West.

This European view of the Orient is illustrated by the books of Karl May (Karl Friedrich May, 1842-1912), the author of many books about the cowboy Old Shatterhand and the Indian Winnetou. Less well-known is the fact that he also wrote books about the Middle East and German East Africa. In these books his hero has the name of Kara ben Nemsi, and he is assisted by his right-hand man, the Muslim Haji Halef Omar. In one of his books May sketches an abominable picture of pitiless Islamic-Arabic slave traders who ruthlessly pursue blacks in the Sudan and exterminate them.

In his books Karl May shows deep knowledge of the Arabs, Islam and the Koran. He regularly quotes from the Koran. But the dominant picture is that of western superiority embodied in Kara ben Nemsi who is described as someone close to a saint. He knows the situation in the Sudan better than the local sheik, although all this knowledge was gained from books he read in Europe.[27] The Arab slave traders "quote the Koran left and right … but they are thieves, and betrayal is commonplace among them."[28] They practice magic, and the *fakir* (Sufi ascetic and, according to May, magician) determines the day when the slave raids may be started. Then they raise the *barakha*, the holy flag on which the Arabic creed is embroidered.[29] All Muslims are really unreliable. Says Kara ben Nemsi:

> If I were a follower of the prophet, you would probably have received nothing; then I would just have filled my own pockets. I am no Muslim.[30]

That is the dominant picture Karl May presents of Muslims. Fortunately, there are also a few noble Muslims. At the death of one of these, Kara ben Nemsi says the following prayer:

> Allah is Allah! There is but one God and we all are his children.... Dust now goes into the earth. His [the deceased's] countenance turns to

Mecca, the Golden City; but his soul stands before the Most Merciful and beholds his Glory, where no mortal eye can penetrate. His is life; ours is the consolation that we also will one day stand at his side, on the day when Isa ben Maryam shall come to judge the living and the dead.[31]

That is quite remarkable. The European Christian says an Islamic prayer! And he knows that Jesus (Isa ben Maryam) will come at the end of time as the final judge.

However, Karl May is extremely negative when he speaks about Islamic mysticism, at least that of the whirling Dervishes. Kara ben Nemsi attends such a Dervish dance in Istanbul and has the following to say:

> The monks are usually married and, besides their joint services, they spend their days in idleness eating, drinking, sleeping, playing and smoking. In old times the Dervishes had great influence; today, however, they are no longer as much respected and only the common people continue to honor them. For this reason they practice certain arts through which they make it appear as if they are the chosen ones and can perform miracles. They perform all kinds of clever stunts and present shows in which they perform strange dances or sing plaintive songs.[32]

This negative judgment of Sufi mysticism is no exception. We will see later that H. P. Blavatsky said similar things.

Political Discussion

After the French-German War in 1870, the king of Prussia was made Emperor of Germany. It was only then that the many German duchies, princedoms, etc., were combined into one state. The fact that this occurred so late had the result that Germany was a latecomer in the European hunt for colonies. France had colonized Algeria already in 1830, and the Russians and the British were active in Afghanistan already in 1840. The queen of England was made Empress of British India (India, Pakistan and Bangladesh) in 1876. The Germans, however, did not begin to hunt for colonies until 1885. They had to be content with the "remainders" in Africa: Namibia, Sudan, Burundi, Rwanda, Tanzania, Togo and Cameroon. There were Muslims in these colonies, especially in East Africa, as we have already seen in the books of Karl May. Now Germany came into serious contact with local Muslims for the first time.

THE IMPULSE OF FREEDOM IN ISLAM

In 1898, the German emperor Wilhelm II (1859-1941) declared during his journey through the Ottoman Empire that he was a friend and protector of Muslims. At that time, in comparison with England, France and Russia, Germany hardly knew anything of the Muslim world. The relations between Germany and the Ottoman Empire were most cordial. Wilhelm wrote in 1908:

> For years I have warned against riding roughshod over Islam and challenging it, and in all of Europe I have been mocked as being Turk-crazy.... In spite of all my warnings they [the Russian and English politicians] have in their foolish narrow-mindedness and unprecedented overestimation of themselves despised, ill-treated and insulted Islam, until Islam could not take it any more.... Now one more outside intervention with reform proposals, and the sultan of the prophet will unfurl green flags and the cry "Allah" will sound in every corner of Asia and Africa, and that will be the end of the Christians....[33]

A nice piece of German *Realpolitik*. And it worked! During the First World War the Turks were allied with Germany. On November 14, 1914, the Turks proclaimed *jihad* against England and France, and Wilhelm kept his promise: when during the First World War Islamic prisoners of war were interned in Germany, Wilhelm founded the first German mosque in Berlin. It was dedicated in June 1915. Several imams were connected with it, for the total number of Islamic prisoners during the war amounted to no less than 15,000 men.[34]

There were two prevalent views in Europe: "the danger of Islam" and "the potential of Islam." The view of "the danger" was fed by Christian missionaries, while that of "the potential" came from a consideration of economic possibilities. For the missionaries Islam was the worst enemy they could imagine. They often criticized what they called the pro-Islamic policies of European countries, and no one paid enough attention to the slave trade of the Muslims. The missionaries regarded Islam as decadent and void of culture—in truth, Islam is not really a faith, for the only true faith is Christianity, isn't it? Islam is all about war (jihad). The religious fanaticism of Islam is a threat to (Christian) colonial policies. During the *World Missionary Colonial Congress* in 1910 in Edinburgh German missionaries said among other things:

> Islam is an impediment to spiritual progress, and it strengthens fatalism, superstition and magic. Islam permits polygamy and has no concept of the value of physical labor.[35]

Such views were not unique to missionaries; they were supported by influential scientists such as professor Carl Mirbt in his important book *Mission und Kolonialpolitik*[36] and by professor Martin Hartmann, the prominent expert of Oriental studies in Berlin.

But not everyone was so negative. For instance, there was professor Carl Heinrich Becker who taught Oriental studies in Hamburg, who argued that Islam should be seen as an ally. During his speech at the *World Missionary Colonial Congress* he did not make much of all those so-called dangers of Islam. Nevertheless, he regarded Islam as a lagging culture. He called for serious study of Islam in the German colonies. Such studies were made, and the conclusions were rather thin (as were the studies by the way) but did not support the fears of the "threat of Islam."[37]

Literary Discussion: Goethe

It is noteworthy that the German idealists, such as Goethe and Schelling a century earlier, had a remarkably positive picture of Islam,[38] especially Goethe (1749-1832) who had great sympathy for Islam in general and for Sufism in particular. As a young man he wanted to study Oriental cultures, but his father told him to study law. He was fascinated by travel reports of Europeans in the Orient. At the time when he wrote his poems *Die West-Östliche Divan* he learned to read and write Arabic. About the Arabic language he wrote: "In no other language are the spirit, the word and the script united in such an elementary manner."[39]

Goethe read from the Koran to the ruling family of Weimar in the translation by Von Hammer (see below). Schiller was among his listeners. About the Koran Goethe wrote:

> Whether the Koran is from eternity? I don't ask myself that question!...
> Because it is the Book of Books. I believe that out of Muslim duty.[40]

Goethe was particularly interested in the mysticism of Islam. In 1812 Von Hammer translated the collected poems entitled the *Diwan* by the Islamic mystic Hafez (c.1326-c.1391). Goethe was in seventh heaven when he read these. The immediate result was his own cycle of poems *Die West-Östliche Divan*, which was published in 1819 and contains no less than twelve books. The main figures in this cycle are Hatem and his wife Suleika. Goethe also read the works of Rumi (1207-1273) and many other Islamic authors. Evidently he was so fascinated by Islam that his friends sometimes thought he was a Muslim, and ... he did not mind! He said: "... It is an Islam such as sooner or later we will all have to confess."[41]

It was not only Islamic poetry that interested him, but also the Muslim faith. The unity of Allah and his presence in nature and creation appeared again and again in his work. He abhorred the Christian cross. He viewed Jesus (and the other prophets) in the same way as the Koran. And it is self-evident that Mohammed receives high praise from Goethe. In 1772 already he began to compose a play with the title *Mahomet*. It was a reaction to Voltaire's play *Le fanatisme ou Mahomet le Prophète*. *Mahomet* never got beyond fragments but his song of praise to Mohammed is famous: *Mahomets Gesang* (Mohammed's Song).

The love for Islam and Sufism of Goethe and his entourage in Weimar are completely lost a century later. The superiority of Europe and colonial politics have then taken its place.

SCIENTIFIC DISCUSSION

As early as 1613 a professorship in Arabic was established at the University of Leiden, Netherlands, and in 1641 the first Dutch translation of the Koran appeared which, however, was not from Arabic but from the *Alcoranus Mahometicus*, a German translation made in 1616. In turn, the *Alcoranus Mahometicus* was based on the Italian translation of 1547 published in Venice. The year 1647 saw the first translation from Arabic into French, and in 1734 followed an English translation. The first German one dates from 1771-1772 and was followed by one by Von Hammer in 1811 and by the Oriental scholar Friedrich Rückert in 1888. Rückert also translated a lot of Arabic poetry.

Around 1800 the first scientific studies of Islam were appearing in Europe. Initially, these were predominantly philosophical and historical studies. In Germany, the first big historical study of Islam was published by J. J. O. A. Rühle von Lilienstein: *Zur Geschichte der Araber vor Mohamed*, Berlin, 1836. In 1887 the *Seminar für Orientalische Sprachen* was founded in Berlin. In 1900 there were 57 teachers for Oriental studies at 21 universities. The leader in these studies was Theodor Nöldeke (1836-1930) whose doctoral dissertation was written on the origin of the Koran. He spoke Sanskrit, Turkish, Syrian (Aramaic) and Persian. He wrote a number of books about the Muslim world. Even in 2013 his name must not be absent on the reading list of a serious student of Orientalism. However, Nöldeke knew Islam only from books; because of his fragile health he was unable to travel in the Orient. In his *History of the Koran* he said:

The language is long-winded, dull and prosaic, with eternal repetitions in which the prophet does not shrink from using the exact same words over and over again; with argumentation lacking all sharpness and clarity, which convinces no one who does not already believe in the end result; the stories offer little variety and make the revelations often quite boring.[42]

Nöldeke, and just about every westerner of his time, was unable to deal with the poetical character of the Koran. He judged the Koran by western intellectual standards, and it did not measure up.

Other scholars did have the opportunity to travel extensively through the Orient and Africa. One of these was professor Hans Stumme who taught Arabic and Hamitic languages from 1902 to 1930. He also spoke Swahili. All those years he taught Arabic. Around 1900 Berlin counted more scholars in Islam and Orientalism than London and Paris.

As regards the science of religion we can mention Julius Wellhausen and F. Ulrich. The latter wrote his doctoral dissertation in 1912 on predestination in Islam and Christianity. We will speak more about this in chapter 3. Wellhausen is recognized even today as the originator of modern Bible research. But from 1890 he became more and more interested in the history of Islam, as is reflected in his many publications in which he submitted the Koran to the same detailed scrutiny as the Old Testament. This did not fail to provoke criticism. For the Koran came about in a very short time, while the Old Testament came together over a thousand years. You can't simply analyze the Koran with the same methods.[43] Recently however, today's students of Islam have picked up where Wellhausen left off and argue again for a history of the origin of the Koran (see chapter 2).[44]

Then there is the influential Max Weber (1864-1920), economist, historian and law scholar. He was one of the founders of sociology. For our subject, his studies of the relationships between religion and capitalism are important. Weber was very interested in the influence of religion on the development of capitalism and in the question of how it happened that capitalism developed as it did in western Christianity. What role did Christianity play here? And why did capitalism not develop in this way in the Orient? Did other religions perhaps not offer the same conditions and opportunities?

In order to answer these questions, Weber made a comparison between Confucianism, Hinduism, Buddhism, Judaism, early Christianity and early Islam. Weber called his methodology of a comparative science of religions "the sociology of religions." He grounded his vision of Islam primarily in his reading of the Koran, the *sunna* (the "customs" of Mohammed), and the *sharia* (divine law), as well as on German theological and religious-scientific works.[45] Unfortunately, Weber was unable to complete this large project, so that we do not have a complete view of Islam, but what he left is substantial.

About Allah Weber says that he has the same attributes as the God of the Calvinists: omnipotent, unchanging, just, etc. That is logical, for both views of God are based on the Old Testament. But the "fickle despot" of the Old Testament is softened in Calvinism by the redeeming and merciful God of the New Testament. In Islam that is not the case; and this ultimately leads to fatalism. According to Weber, this has everything to do with the fact that, very soon after its founding by Mohammed, Islam became a religion of fighters and did not have an "inner asceticism," inner development. Of course, there are the Sufis, but Weber does not approve of them. Islam is a religion of fighters, and Islamic society—including its laws—are organized along theocratic lines. According to Weber, that is the reason why a western type of rationalism could not arise in the Orient.[46]

Weber's conclusions have not met with much approval. His critics argue that he takes Calvinistic Christianity as his basis and compares this with early Islam, and thus makes early Islam (Arabian Islam) representative for Islam as a whole. And yet, this is what everyone did at the end of the nineteenth century. When one spoke of Islam, it was the historical Islam that was meant. But that is not the same Islam as that of the twentieth century. The scientific knowledge of Islam in Germany was primarily book knowledge—few people ever met a real Muslim of flesh and blood.

Christian Discussion

Many Christians are clear about one thing: "Islam is the beast from the abyss." That was like common sense around 1900—and also earlier and later! When we google the words "Islam" and "666" we get a discouraging picture. Especially in fundamentalist Christian circles it is almost self-evident that Islam represents the Antichrist. That idea has been around for a long time. In the times of the Crusades in the Middle Ages, Mohammed was often equated with the Antichrist. He was not the only one, of course; heretics, and especially the Cathars, were in the Middle Ages generally seen as the Antichrist or as his precursors.[47] Calvin (1509-1564) wrote that the Turks erected "an idol in place of the true God because they are averse to Christ,"[48] but he did not associate this with the beast or the Antichrist. For Calvin, the "popish church" (the Catholic Church) was the Antichrist. Martin Luther (1483-1546) viewed Mohammed as "a devil and first-born of Satan."[49]

Around 1900 things became more serious. A man by the name of L. R. Conradi (1856-1939), director of the *Internationale Traktatgesellschaft*, wrote a book entitled (translated title) *Mystery Unfolds or The Seven Seals Opened*, published in 1915 in many countries. The *Internationale Traktatgesellschaft* was another name for the Seventh-Day Adventists of that time. The Seventh-Day Adventist Church in Germany was founded by Conradi in 1888 in Hamburg and had as its mission to acquaint everyone with the "glorious gospel of Jesus Christ, even in the dark countries of the heathen."[50] We read the following about Mohammed in the above-mentioned book:

> From the beginning he showed something unhealthy in a spiritual respect. In dreams and hallucinations the child of religion he bore came into the world. The Koran says that he received the key of God so as to unlock the true religion and the heavens. In our text, however, which was given five centuries before Mohammed's time to the holy Apostle John, it is explained which key this was, namely the key of the pit of the abyss; world history has sufficiently confirmed this.[51]

And:

> This angel of the abyss [Rev. 9:11] is the living personification of Islam; he appears in history in the person of Mohammed and the Caliphs, but he really came into his own with the founding of the Ottoman Sultanate.[52]

Many theologians regard Abaddon as the Antichrist or, at any rate, the precursor of the Antichrist.[53] Conradi made a distinction between the Islam of the Arabs and Islam under the Turks. The Turks were much worse. Under Arab Mohammedanism there is freedom of religion. Conradi pointed to the "Church of the Orient," meaning the Christians outside the sphere of influence of the Syrian-Orthodox Church, such as the Nestorians (see chapter 4):

> Under the rule of the Mohammedans, and especially under that of the Arabs, she [the Church of the Orient] was much more fortunate than under the power of the Greek emperors.[54]

Conradi had a great deal of sympathy for the "Church of the Orient" because they were considered heretics by Roman and Syrian-Orthodox Christianity. And thus, by definition, the "Church of the Orient" is good. In Conradi's view, we find the heritage of the "Church of the Orient," mark you, with the Cathars in Europe in the Middle Ages. All these "heretics" were precursors of the Reformation. And the beast from the abyss was, in Conradi's eyes, the Roman Church. His book shows Conradi to be an erudite man. He was well informed about oriental history and the history of Islam. He quoted the Koran and many authors who had the same views on Islam and the Saracens as he had. Evidently, in his book Conradi represented a widely held view. He said: "Ever since Luther, almost all Protestants agree that they [the horsemen who kill a third of humanity, Rev. 9:17-19] are the Mohammedans."[55] He was referring to the Turks. But the Turks were a "scourge of God," and their power "has to be found in our sins and apostasy."[56]

Of course, Conradi was not representative for *the* Christian view of Islam. It is interesting to note how Islam was viewed from a Catholic perspective. The *Catholic Encyclopedia* of 1911 had an article on Islam. The author was well informed and neutral, especially as regards the founding of Islam. But when the subject was Islam as a religion, things changed. For instance, the author wrote about the Islamic view of paradise the following: "The joys and glory of paradise are so fantastic and sensual, as only the voluptuous Arabic spirit can imagine." And about Allah's omnipotence:

> The Mohammedan doctrine of predestination is the same as fatalism. They believe in God's absolute judgment and predestination both for good and for evil.... Everything proceeds from divine will and has been irreversibly fixed for all eternity. The possession and exercise of our own free will is therefore futile and useless. The absurdity of this doctrine was felt by later Mohammedan theologians who have tried in vain to minimize it by diverse subtle distinctions.[57]

By the way, it is striking that the *Catholic Encyclopedia* did report that Islam does not recognize Christ, but nothing was said about the fact that Islam has great respect for Isa (Jesus).

Esoteric Discussion

H. P. Blavatsky and Annie Besant

If we want to answer the question as to how Islam figured in esoteric discussions around the year 1900, we first of all have to consult H. P. Blavatsky (1831-1891) and the Theosophical Society. Around 1900 the Theosophical Society was the "leading lady" in esoteric circles. As a young woman, Blavatsky traveled through the Middle East and met sheiks, Bedouins, and dervishes.[58] She reported that she had an encounter with dervishes in an obscure monastery in a slum of Istanbul and said that their leader took her to the "Oracle of Tatmos," also known under the name of the "Oracle of Damascus." This oracle is a kind of monstrosity, a dwarf with a hideous face. Her forehead had verses of the Koran written on it and she had a crown on her head. The dervish drew a magical circle around the oracle, picked her up by her feet and began his whirling dervish dance. After two minutes he suddenly stopped and put the oracle in its place in the circle. The oracle was now in a deep trance. A mandorla of light formed around the oracle, a vision in which the city of Istanbul became visible. Street after street was shown, and this panorama finally stopped at a specific location, the place where Blavatsky's poor little dog was lying that she had lost.[59]

As to its content, Blavatsky said hardly anything about Islam. In her extensive work there are only a few isolated remarks. In *The Secret Doctrine* she said only that fanatic Muslims view Jesus as a prophet, and that Christians view Mohammed as a false prophet.[60] It seems as if Blavatsky took no special interest in Islam.

Not so with her successor, Annie Besant (1847-1933), who discussed Islam in the context of the unity of world religions in *The Brotherhood of Religions*.[61] In *The Theosophist* of 1901 she wrote the article *The Rising of Islam* and in 1910 *Islam in the Light of Theosophy*. She also gave lectures on Islam, including one in 1932 in India—where there are many Muslims—in which she said some remarkable things. She quoted Sura 4:3 of the Koran in which Mohammed says that a man may have a maximum of four wives, and because of this women in Islam are better off than their counterparts in western Christianity. Polygamy may be outlawed in the West, but the result is "illegal" polygamy: men have mistresses and visit prostitutes. Their women have much less legal protection than in Islam. And this from the former suffragette Besant!

Noteworthy is also her defense against the western view that Islam is not progressive and does not value schooling and science. If that is your opinion, you have not looked at the history of Islam, she says. At a time when science was still unknown in Christianity, Islamic science spread all over Europe (in the tenth and eleventh centuries). The Moors brought science to Europe, including Greek metaphysics, mathematics, astronomy, architecture, "scientific agriculture," and chemistry.[62]

Annie Besant was not the only theosophist with an interest in Islam. For instance, there is a little book from 1927 entitled *Reincarnation and Islam* by Nader Baig Mirza (1891-1940).[63] The author contended that there are sayings in the Koran that point to reincarnation, such as in Sura 2:243: "... Allah said to them, 'Die;'

again He gave them life; most surely Allah is Gracious to people...." And there is the book by C. G. Harrison from 1894, *The Transcendental Universe*.⁶⁴ This book describes (the esoteric approach to) the evolution of the world. It is popular in theosophical circles.⁶⁵ In chapter 5 Harrison wrote:

> Mohammedans have a tradition that comes close to the truth, namely that the Garden of Eden was situated in the middle region between the earth and the moon.

Finally we should note that in his influential book *The Great Initiates* the French theosophist Édouard Schuré discussed Rama, Krishna, Hermes, Moses, Orpheus, Pythagoras, Plato and Jesus, but not Mohammed.

Rudolf Steiner

As opposed to Besant, Rudolf Steiner (1861-1925) had little good to say about Islam. That is strange, because Steiner was the leader of the German Theosophical Society for some ten years, and he was also strongly influenced by Goethe. He worked for seven years at the Goethe and Schiller Archives in Weimar. In these archives the intensive studies Goethe made of the Koran in 1771-1772 and later are preserved. The international center of the anthroposophists in Dornach, Switzerland, is called The Goetheanum. We have already seen how enthusiastic Goethe was about Islam and especially Islamic mysticism. But Steiner never even mentioned Sufism.

In September 1924 Rudolf Steiner gave a course for the priests of The Christian Community in which he discussed the Apocalypse of St. John. In 1995 these lectures were published in German, followed by an English translation in 1998 entitled *The Book of Revelation and the Work of the Priest*. In the foreword to the Dutch translation the editors wrote: "The content of these lectures is so profound, so prophetic, and after eighty years still so timely, that it is of great significance for anyone who wishes to interpret the signs of the time."⁶⁶ In the lectures of September 11 and 12, 1924, Steiner spoke about the number of the beast, 666. The significance of this number for Steiner was simply the year 666 AD. That was an important year, in which "what lives in Arabism, in Mohammedanism, sprang up everywhere."⁶⁷

Based on the above, however, we may conclude that Steiner was in this case not at all profound or prophetic—he largely followed the popular, scientific and Christian patterns of discussion of Islam in his time. This is notable in almost all Steiner's lectures in which he speaks of Islam. For instance, he characterized

Islam as fatalistic: "Allah predestines everything,"[68] although he also said that the problem of free will and predestination can be found just as well in Christianity.[69] All in all we must observe on the basis of a study of all Steiner's statements on Islam, Mohammedanism, Arabism and the Koran, that his wisdom is often encyclopedic. Sometimes however, Steiner proved to be well-informed, for instance, when he pointed out that the Islam of Mohammed and the Arabs is a totally different Islam than that which developed as a result of the conquests of the Seljuks (Turks) around the year 1000 (see chapter 2). Compared with Seljuk Islam, there positively exists a freedom impulse in Arabic Islam. The fatalistic and determinist nature of Islam arose only with the Seljuks, even if a basic tendency in that direction was already present in the Koran, according to Steiner.[70]

In one respect Rudolf Steiner seems to be unique for his time. This is when he puts great emphasis on the role of Isa (Jesus) in Islam. First of all, it is Isa who brings the freedom impulse in Islam[71] (but not to the same extent as in Christianity); second, the Isa of the Koran is the so-called Nathan Jesus.[72] Steiner makes a distinction between Jesus as described in the Gospel of St. Luke (the Nathan Jesus) and Jesus as described in the Gospel of St. Matthew (the Solomon Jesus). According to Steiner, Muslims have often developed more understanding of the Nathan Jesus than many Christians:

> So speaks this document [the Koran] about Jesus, of whom in this case only the one manifestation is taken into account. Could we not say of this document that those who believe in it, believe substantially more than many who not only call them themselves Christians today, but teach Christianity because of their profession? Don't those who firmly believe in this document, believe much more of Christianity than some of those who today often call themselves teachers of Christianity? And please do not think that I read to you from some document—perhaps you know it—that is regarded by a few people, a small sect, as the true witness for their faith! I read this to you from the Koran, and every Turk believes everything it says in this 19th Sura. This is proof therefore, that numerous people among us who call themselves Christians don't even know and believe enough of Christianity to call themselves Turks!... They should realize that a Turk believes more of Christianity than they do.[73]

The problem in evaluating Rudolf Steiner is that his work is so immense in volume that it is far from simple to place his statements in context. This is also true for what he said about Islam. Many judgments on Islam are passed in exactly the same way on Christianity. For instance, Steiner said that Islam is based on the strictly monotheistic Father God as the primal creative power. But he said precisely the same thing about Christianity of his time.[74] We will review Steiner's statements in greater detail in chapter 4.

G. I. Gurdjieff

Rudolf Steiner's "occult" wisdom about Islam was largely based on a western point of view. In this regard he was a product of the colonial picture. Other occultists of his time knew Islam from the inside; G. I. Gurdjieff (1872-1949) was one of these. Gurdjieff was born in Alexandropol, Russia (Armenia), on the Turkish border. After the Russian-Turkish War of 1877 his parents moved to the conquered Turkish city of Kars. According to his hagiographers he traveled in the Middle East: Afghanistan, Persia, Egypt and the Holy Land. In 1910 Gurdjieff settled down in Moscow. In 1921 he moved to Western Europe where he gave lectures and demonstrations in Berlin, and then took up permanent residence in Paris where he died in 1949.

He said that in 1897 he studied with a Sufi master in Afghanistan, who brought him into contact with a Sarmouni monastery where the Enneagram is practiced. For the Sarmouni's the Enneagram is an important medium to make divine predictions and achieve personal transformation. Later the Enneagram became an important part of the spiritual teaching of Gurdjieff's School of Enlightenment. He visited Medina and Mecca, but traditional Islam did not appeal to him. For this reason he sought contact with the Naqshbandi Sufi order.* Gurdjieff's esoteric teaching was inspired by this Sufi order. But he was also influenced by Theosophy. In the West, the Enneagram was introduced in 1949 by P. Ouspensky (1878-1947), the most important pupil and coworker of Gurdjieff.[75]

Muhammed Iqbal

To the extent mystical Islam was known in Europe around 1900, this came about principally through Muslims from India, such as Muhammed Iqbal (1876-1938). Iqbal was a philosopher, politician and poet. He was already a famous poet in the Punjab (Pakistan) before he started his studies in Europe. He studied law in

---

* Translator's note: The Naqshbandi order is the only Sufi order that claims to trace its direct spiritual lineage/chain (*silsilah*) to the Islamic prophet Muhammad, through Abu Bakr, the first Caliph and Muhammad's companion. (Source: Wikipedia)

Cambridge and earned his doctorate in Munich in 1907 with a dissertation on the philosophy of Persian metaphysicians. He described in detail the spiritual development of the human being and the journey of the human soul after death through the diverse spiritual regions as described in Persian literature. But he also referred to Dante. Iqbal was strongly influenced by western philosophers such as Friedrich Nietzsche, Henri Bergson and Hegel. But his greatest admiration was for Goethe. Iqbal was very critical of western materialism and expressed this in his poems *Pegham-e-Mahriq* (Message from the East), in the first line of which he referred to Goethe. His philosophical work *The Reconstruction of Religious Thought in Islam* (1930) became a bestseller. He is regarded as the intellectual "Founding Father" of Pakistan.[76]

HAZRAT INAYAT KHAN

While we may wonder whether Muhammed Iqbal can be called a "true" mystic, for Hazrat Inayat Khan (1882-1927) this is not a question. We know Inayat Khan primarily because he founded the first Sufi order in Europe, headquartered in the little town of Katwijk, Netherlands. Khan was also a Muslim from North India. He was very musical and often brought his message of universal mysticism in the form of music. From 1900 to 1903 he taught music at the music academy of Baroda, North India. Between 1903 and 1907 he studied with a Sufi master and was initiated as a Muslim mystic. In 1910 he travelled with a group of musicians to America and Europe to give concerts of Indian music. In 1913 he married the American Ora Ray Baker, and in the same year appeared his first mystical book *Sufi Message of Spiritual Liberty*, published by the Theosophical Publishing House. During the First World War the music group was in England where they had many contacts with theosophists. Khan's message of universal mysticism is much more related to Theosophy than to the classical Sufi orders of the Orient. From this time the Sufi movement of Inayat Khan began to grow. In 1922 Khan established himself and his movement in Geneva and started the work in Katwijk. He also spoke six times in Germany. In 1923 Khan called on the influential Swedish Lutheran Archbishop of Uppsala, Nathan Söderblom (1866-1931), who was a scholar of Islam (in 1930 he received the Nobel Peace Prize). Khan also received an audience from the pope. He then returned to India for reasons of health, and died there in his forty-fifth year.[77] By then the Sufi movement had taken root in Europe.

Conclusion

Edward Wadi Said was right. Whether we are looking at the popular, scientific, religious or esoteric discussion, generally around the beginning of the twentieth century the image of Islam was very negative. And it has not become much better since! The West may have thrown off its military-political colonialism, but its economic-cultural colonialism is still in full swing.

Chapter 2

History of Islam

When we speak of "Islam," which Islam do we really mean? The Islam of Indonesia? Or that of the Berbers in Algeria? Islam shows different faces, not only in geography but also in history. The early Islam of the Arabs in the seventh century is different from the Islam after the conquests of the Seljuks around the year 1000. And what was in existence before Mohammed and the rise of Islam? Here is a brief history.

Christian Arabs Before Islam

From the middle of the third century CE the Sassanids were ruling in the Greater Syrian region. Under Khosrau I (531-579) and Khosrau II (591-628) the Sassanid realm greatly expanded to include Palestine and Egypt. The Sassanids were the archenemies of Rome and later of Byzantium. In 622 the Sassanids suffered a crushing defeat at the hands of the Byzantines. In 675 the tide turned and the Sassanids devastated the Byzantines.

The eastern border of today's Syria was the more or less permanent border between the Sassanid and Roman/Byzantine empires. In this period (third to seventh century) we speak of Greater Syria which consisted of West Syria (roughly equal to today's Syria) and East Syria (extending approximately to Baghdad). In history books we can read about many wars between the Sassanids and the Romans/Byzantines. What is usually not mentioned is that these wars were in fact fought by Arabic vassals of the Sassanids and Rome/Byzantium, respectively the Lakhmids and the Ghassanids. Long before the great Islamic-Arabic conquests there were already Arabic tribes in West and East Syria. Who were they?

Lakhmids and Ghassanids

In the realm of the Sassanids the state religion was Zoroastrianism. Khosrau II, however, was married to the Byzantine-Christian princess Maria and the Syrian-Christian Shirin. His finance minister, Yazdin, was a Christian. Khosrau protected the Nestorian-Christian Church. Next to his palace in Seleucia stood a Nestorian church. Christian Manichaeism, however, was persecuted.

There were Arabic tribes in the Sassanid realm. They formed vassal states on the border with the Byzantines. The best known among these tribes is that of the Lakhmids, who had migrated to Iraq out of the Arabian peninsula already in the third century. Their capital was Hira on the west bank of the Euphrates. Reports from about the year 300 tell us that they were Nestorians, Christians therefore. Hira had a Nestorian Episcopal see. It was a cultural center, and there seem to be indications that it was in Hira that the Arabic script was developed.

Around 422 the Lakhmids were powerful and had influence on the Sassanid kings. They participated in wars against the Romans and Byzantines, in which their king Munhir III (died 554) was commander in chief of the Sassanids. Munhir conducted peace negotiations, and later conquered Palestine—read: the Sassanids under Khosrau II conquered Palestine in 614. Medina on the Arabian Peninsula was controlled by Munhir III. In 575 the kingdom of the Lakhmids fell because the Ghassanids (i.e., the Byzantines) conquered Hira.

At the same time there were Arab vassal states of Byzantium in West Syria: the Ghassanids who had come from south Arabia. They also began their migration to the north in the third century. In the sixth century they were incorporated in the Byzantine Empire and functioned as border guards and vassal states in the province of Syria. At that time they converted to Christianity, but of a different flavor than the Lakhmids; the Ghassanids became Monophysites. Their state (as vassal state) flourished under Arethas (529-559) and his son al-Mundir (569-581).

We may conclude from this that the migrations of Arabic tribes from the Arabian Peninsula to surrounding areas had already begun in the third century.

Thus around 600 we see the following situation:

> East Syria: the Arabic Nestorian-Christian vassal state of the Lakhmids under the Sassanids; the official state religion was Zoroastrianism;
> West Syria: the Arabic Monophysite-Christian vassal state of the Ghassanids under Byzantium; the official state religion was orthodox Syrian/Byzantine Christianity.

The wars between the Sassanids and the Byzantines were fought primarily between these two Arabic vassal states.

From 604 on, Khosrau II of the Sassanids gradually conquered Syria, Palestine (614) and Egypt (617). In consequence, the West Syrian Arabs were now joined with the East Syrian Arabs under the Sassanids. The Ghassanids received more (Monophysite) religious freedom and turned against Byzantium. A reaction had to come: in 622 the Sassanids suffered a crushing defeat, after which the old borders were reinstated. But the consequence of all those wars between the Sassanids and Byzantium was that both empires became exhausted. A power vacuum developed in West and East Syria of which the Arabian leaders made good use.

Four Honorable Caliphs[78]

When Mohammed died in 632, his father-in-law Abu Bakr (572-634) was chosen as his successor (Caliph). Mohammed's cousin, Ali, was not present when this happened. Abu Bakr was the father of Aisha, one of Mohammed's wives. He united all the Arabian tribes and conquered Syria and Mesopotamia. It is said that Abu Bakr and Ali transmitted the esoteric teaching that was later called *Tassawuf* or Sufism.

After Abu Bakr's death Umar ibn al-Khattab (592-644) was chosen as his successor. Umar's daughter Hafsa was also one of Mohammed's wives. He was very strict and was murdered in 644. He conquered Palestine (with Jerusalem) in 634, and Egypt in 639-642. The Persian kingdom of the Sassanids suffered bad defeats and was finally conquered by Umar's successor, Uthman ibn Affan (574-656).

Uthman was successively married to two daughters of Mohammed. He came from a wealthy family in Mecca, the Umayyads, who belonged to the tribe of the Quraish. Mohammed's family, the Hashemites, also belonged to the Quraish, but a different branch. Uthman converted to Islam as a young man, which is noteworthy because there existed an age-old rivalry in Mecca between the Umayyads and the Hashemites. The issue in this rivalry was the question of which clan should lead the Quraish and would therefore be the guardians of the Kaaba. Uthman participated in the first Muslim migration to the city of Aksum in northern Ethiopia and in the later move from Mecca to Medina.[79] In Islamic tradition Uthman was one of the ten people who were destined for paradise. The fact that he was chosen by the Muslims means therefore that this choice transcended clan connections. But not everyone was happy with that. For, conversion to Islam means breaking traditional tribal connections.

Uthman was murdered in 656 because of discord in respect of taxation. After his death Ali ibn Abi Talib (c.600-661) was chosen as the last of the "four honorable Caliphs." His father was Abu Talib,[80] but he was adopted and brought up by Mohammed whose daughter Fatima he then married. According to some traditions he was present when Mohammed received his revelations in the cave of Hira. His election as the fourth Caliph was opposed by the ambitious and competent general Muawiyah, governor of Syria, who belonged to the Umayyad clan. In 661 Ali was murdered by order of Muawiyah, the event that resulted in the division between the Shiites (Ali) and the Sunnites (Umayyads). This division is strongly rooted in culture: in the opinion of some people the succession should be arranged within Mohammed's family; others think that this should be decided by the Quraish tribe.

The Umayyads

In 634 Syria was conquered under the second Caliph Umar from Medina. In 638 the Umayyads conquered Jerusalem, and in 642 they assumed supreme power in the expanding Arab empire. That is the year 20 of the Hijra*, the beginning of the Islamic era. In 675 the Umayyads had reached Constantinople.

In order to bolster the power of the Umayyad dynasty they needed not only military supremacy, but also religious legitimacy. For that reason the founder of the dynasty, Caliph Muawiyah, placed the political and religious center of his power in Damascus, the sanctuary of John the Baptist. Coins from Damascus in that time show pictures of a cross. Through his connection with the prophet John the Baptist, Muawiyah obtained more authority over the Arabic tribes in Syria (the Ghassanids), for they had been Christians for a long time. There are coins on which the Christian Arabic rulers are pictured as *Agnus Dei*, the Lamb of God. Nestorians, but also orthodox Christians, occupied important posts at the court of the Umayyads. In view of all these facts, one could well wonder whether the Umayyads really were Muslims. The Byzantine theologian John Damascene (died 735) called the Arabic conquerors Christian heretics. He called them Ishmaelites, after Ishmael, the other son of Abraham from which the Arabs say they have descended.

Coins from early Umayyad times sometimes have the words *abd Allah*, "Servant of God" (Allah = God in both Arabic and Aramaic). The ruler gave himself this

---

* Translator's note: The *Hijra* is the migration or journey of the prophet Mohammed and his followers from Mecca to Medina in 622 CE. (Source: Wikipedia)

predicate. It did not refer to the name of the ruler as such but was rather a spiritual honorific. The name of the physical father was not mentioned. That is unusual. There are also coins with the letters *MHMT,* meaning *Muhammad*. But here the name of the father of the ruler is also missing. The word *Muhammad* was also an honorific and did not refer to the person of Mohammed. If that had been so, his father would have had to be mentioned. With *Muhammad*, Jesus would have been meant, the Praised One. That was the motto with which the Umayyads wanted to forge the Arabic realm into a religious unity. Under the flag of Jesus they tried to achieve religious unity. In this way a Mohammedanism grew which was still a mixture of Christianity and early Islam. This is the opinion of the numismatist Volker Popp.[81]

THE ABBASIDS—MUSLIMS

In the year 131 of the *Hijra* (753 CE) a coin first appeared with a different honorific: *Abu Muslim*. This is the first time we hear of Muslims, representatives of Islam. A Muslim is someone who confesses Islam. Evidently a change is brewing. This was connected with the rise of a new Arabic dynasty, the Abbasids. The Abbasids were an Arabic tribe that conquered the Persian empire—the old Sassanid realm—in the seventh century. The founder of this dynasty was Abul Abbas al-Saffah, Caliph of Baghdad 750-754. In his opinion, only the descendants of Hashim, grandfather of Mohammed, had the right to be Caliph. It is only at this time, some one hundred years after Mohammed's death, that Mohammedanism began to be oriented on Mohammed. Was it only at this point that Islam developed as we know it?

Abul Abbas al-Saffah (the shedder of blood) defeated the Umayyads at Kufa in 750, with the result that the capital of the Arab empire was moved to Baghdad. The next Abbasid Caliph was Harun al-Rashid (Caliph 786-809), friend of Charlemagne. It is said that in the year 803 Harun made a pilgrimage to Mecca in order to demonstrate that he was the protector of the Kaaba. Harun's son, al-Mamun, called himself *imam* and *Khalifatullah* (Allah's representative on earth), expressing in this way that he was both secular and spiritual leader.

In Baghdad there was a hodgepodge of religions at that time. There were Jews with their Torah, Manichaeans with their canon of seven books, East Syrian Christians with their *Diatessaron* (a combination of the four gospels into one single narrative created by Tatian circa 160-175), Zoroastrians and Buddhists.

All these religions had their "book," only the Muslims did not. Until that time, the Koran was never mentioned in any Arabic writing. What did exist was a kind of "primal" Koran amid a rich variety of apocryphal and other (Christian) scripture. But only at the end of the second century of the *Hijra* did the Koran become the one and only authoritative scripture of Islam. Just like the Old and New Testaments, the Koran also has a history of coming into being.

Then it will not surprise us any more that the first surviving biography of Mohammed, the *Sirat sayyidina Muhammad rasul Allah* by Ibn Hisham (died 834), was written some 200 years after Mohammed's death. Naturally, this biography is based on older oral material, which is why it is not always clear whether a story is historically accurate or reflects a legend. This is the biography that developed the images of Mohammed and Islam that we now have.

Islam as we know it is the work of the Abbasid al-Mamun. He brought the entire region, as far as Egypt, under "his" interpretation of Mohammedanism: Islam. *Muhammad* is no longer Jesus but the historical Mohammed.[82] At least, this is the view of the so-called "revisionist" school. Naturally this view stands diametrically opposite to the tradition that Mohammed received the Koran in its entirety as a revelation during his life. The truth probably lies somewhere in between.

The Inscription on the Dome of the Rock in Jerusalem

The idea that Islam grew into *the* Islam only under al-Mamun is of course a problematic interpretation, especially in view of the fact that in the famous Dome of the Rock in Jerusalem there is an inscription in golden letters that reads as follows:

> Muhammad(un) 'abd(u)-llah(i) wa-rasuluh(u) ... / ya-'ahl(a) l-kitab(i) la teghlu fi dinikum wa-la taqulu 'ala-llah(i) 'illa l-haqq(a) / in(na)ma l-Masih(u) 'Isa ibn(u) Maryam resul(u)-llah(i). (Sura 4:171)[83]

Translation:

> O followers of the Book! do not exceed the limits in your religion, and do not speak [lies] against Allah, but [speak] the truth; the Messiah, Isa son of Maryam, is only an apostle of Allah.

ISLAM IN HISTORICAL AND THEOLOGICAL PERSPECTIVE

This text was inscribed during the construction in the year 72 of the *Hijra* (694 CE) by the Umayyads; yet it looks like the classical Arabic of the Koran. But is that really so? In view of all we have described in the previous sections of this chapter, we could also read:

> Praiseworthy (*Muhammad(un)*) is the servant of God who is his apostle....
> Christ (*Masih*), Jesus (*Isa*), son of Mary, is God's apostle.

In that case, the apostle of Allah is not Mohammed but Jesus Christ. Was that what the Umayyads intended? When the Abbasid ruler al-Mamun visited the Dome of the Rock in Jerusalem in 832 (138 years later), he read:

> Mohammed, the servant of God, who is his apostle.

Al-Mamun restored the Dome of the Rock, including the inscription, and made a number of changes. He put his own name in the place of that of the Umayyad builder, Caliph Abd al-Malik, and who knows what else he may have changed out of his Islamic ideology?[84] But many people disagree with this interpretation, including well-known Islamologists.

THE SELJUKS

The next great wave of conquerors was that of the Seljuks, who were named after their khan Seljuk (around 1000). They belonged to a Turkish group of tribes called Oghuz-Turks. Together with other tribes—the Kipchaks and the Uighurs—they formed the Götük kingdom which stretched from East Turkestan (in Mongolia) to the Caspian Sea. In the ninth century, the Seljuks occupied areas in today's Kazakhstan and Uzbekistan. They were Christians (Manichaeans?) but around 960 they converted to Islam. In 1030 they conquered Khorasan (in central Asia), and in the battle of Dandanqan in 1040 they defeated the Gaznavids (originally part of the Tajiks, a Persian group that originated in Khorasan—Rumi was a Tajik). Around 1055 they defeated the Buyids in western Persia, which meant that they in fact became the rulers of the Abbasid Caliphate in Baghdad. A son of Seljuk, Tugrul Bek, received the title of Sultan from the Caliph in Baghdad.

Under the Seljuk leader Alp Arslan (1060-1072) Anatolia in Turkey was conquered from the Byzantines in the battle of Manzikert in 1071. Syria had already been conquered the year before, bringing under Seljuk rulership Mecca and Medina, which at that time were held by the Shiite Fatamids of the independent Caliphate in Egypt. The Sharif of Mecca[85] recognized the sovereignty of Alp Arslan. Under Alp Arslan and his successor Malik Shah I (1072-1092), and in the East the Persian vizier Nizam al-Mulk (1065-1092), the Seljuk Sultanate reached its political and cultural culmination. At the same time, the Kerman Seljuks occupied Oman in the southeast corner of the Arabian Peninsula.

Islam as practiced by the Seljuks is not the same as the Islam of the Arabs. Arab Islam is more intellectual than Seljuk Islam. The famous Arab philosopher Averroes (1126-1198) could be considered exemplary for Arab Islam. In due course his works were banned under the influence of another great philosopher, Al-Ghazali (1058-1111). Al-Ghazali is often called in Islam the "Seal of the Philosophers." He was born in Khorasan and was the architect of Seljuk Islam. He rejected intellectual Islam and preached a kind of mystic Islam. His book *Ihya ulum al-din* (*The Revival of the Religious Sciences*) had enormous influence. In essence, this book says that prayers and rituals are able to provide more knowledge of God than intellectual work (more on this in chapter 3).

The Crusades

For centuries Christian pilgrims had visited Jerusalem without any trouble from the Arab Muslims. That changed under the Seljuks, who had conquered Syria in 1070 and Anatolia in 1071, exactly the areas the pilgrims had to traverse on their way to Jerusalem. Only now did problems begin to arise and were the pilgrims harassed by the Muslims—the Seljuks. The pilgrims therefore had to be protected, and this was the motive for the Crusades. The First Crusade was proclaimed by the pope in Rome in 1096. The Arab Muslims were, one could say, ground to dust between the onrushing Turks from the East and the Crusaders from the West. In 1099 the Crusaders conquered Jerusalem on the "Saracens." Among other things, they founded the Crusader state of Edessa in Syria, but this lasted only until 1144 when it was reconquered by the Seljuks. One of the most famous Muslim ruler-generals in the age of the Crusades was Saladin (1138-1193), who founded the Ayyubid dynasty in Egypt. He was not a Seljuk but a Kurd. In due course he managed to concentrate all power in the Muslim world into his person and declared himself independent of the Seljuks. In 1187 he conquered Jerusalem from the Crusaders and Templars.

ISLAM IN HISTORICAL AND THEOLOGICAL PERSPECTIVE

Genghis Khan

Not long after this a new wave of Turks arose in the East: the Mongols of Genghis Khan (1162-1227), who united a host of Mongolian tribes in 1215 and had his capital in Peking. Between 1218 and 1224 he conquered all of Central Asia, Afghanistan, Persia and eastern Europe. In a great battle in 1223 at the Kalka river (Ukraine), Khan defeated the army of Prince Mstislav of Kiev and his allies. From there he conducted raids into the West rather than real conquests. Khan persecuted no one because of their religion; he believed in religious freedom. He conquered part of Anatolia but did not reach Syria and the Arabian Peninsula. The skirmishes of the Crusaders and Byzantines with the Muslims continued to be with the Seljuks.

The Ottomans or Turks

The power of the Seljuks began to crumble around 1250, and the empire was divided up into independent *beyliks* (regions governed by a bey). One of these was the Osman Beylik where in 1280 Osman I came to power. He started to increase his power in Asia Minor. At this point we can begin to speak of Ottomans. They conquered Constantinople in 1453, and in 1517 they also conquered part of western Arabia, including Mecca, although in actual fact the Sharifs continued to protect Mecca. From the beginning of the sixteenth century all of West Central Asia, the Arabian Peninsula, Egypt, Syria, Palestine, Asia Minor, Greece, Bulgaria and Rumania were parts of the "Ottoman Kingdom."

Persia (Iran) remained independent under a variety of dynasties. From 1501 to 1736 the Safavids were ruling Persia. They were originally Turkish Sufis, and they turned Persia into a Shiite state. Other dynasties followed after 1736 until in 1923 the Cossack general Reza Khan proclaimed himself Shah of Persia in a coup d'etat. He founded the Pahlavi dynasty of which the second and last shah was expelled in the revolution of Ayatollah Khomeini in 1979.

Around 1500 Afghanistan, Turkmenistan, Uzbekistan and Kazakhstan (the areas of the old Turks) were conquered by another Turkic tribe, the Timurs. For centuries a variety of Turkic tribes fought each other there for dominance. In the beginning of the eighteenth century the Pashtuns emerged as a strong force; they are still today the largest group of the population of Afghanistan. In 1747 the leader of the Pashtuns proclaimed himself king, and Afghanistan became an independent kingdom centered in Kandahar and Kabul. Despite this, however, tribal wars and warlords continued to dominate politics, and the influence of the Russians and British kept growing (see below).

Colonialism

From the middle of the nineteenth century the Europeans started to arrive in the Muslim world. Afghanistan was a British possession on and off from 1840. It took three Anglo-Afghan wars, but the British never did achieve a definitive victory—not much seems to have changed since then! In the middle of the nineteenth century Iran came under the influence of Russia and England. Parts of the Arabian peninsula came under British influence, and Oman even became a British colony. In 1882 Egypt became a British protectorate. Northern Iran, Turkmenistan, Uzbekistan and Kazakhstan were conquered by Russia between 1865 and 1876. Because of all these colonial actions the Ottomans lost piece after piece of their empire, and in the eyes of the West it became "the sick old man of Europe." Moreover, in the First World War the Ottoman Empire sided with the Germans, in consequence of which it lost large areas in the peace treaty of Versailles in 1918.

The First World War also had consequences for Mecca. Sharif Hussein ibn Ali (1853-1931), king of the kingdom of Hejaz (in the western part of Saudi Arabia), initially sided with the Ottomans, but Lawrence of Arabia managed to lure him to the British side in exchange for an independent kingdom after the end of the war. But in 1924 already the Wahhabi—the royal family of the Saudi kings—conquered Arabia. The Wahhabi are far more puritanical than the Sharifs were.

Conclusion

In the course of history Islam has changed color, character and nuance many times. One cannot speak of *the* Islam, as if Islam as Mohammed intended it had remained unchanged for fourteen centuries. Different Arabic tribes gave different faces to Islam, and the color the Seljuks gave it was different again. The initial freedom impulse of Mohammed has perhaps been snowed under in the course of centuries. The same thing happened in Christianity. That is the subject of the next chapter.

CHAPTER 3

Allah: Predestination or Freedom?

The Islamic creed (*shahadah*) is as follows: *ashhadu an lā ilaha illā-llah, ashhadu anna muhammada rasūlu-llah*. It means: "I witness that there is no God but God, I witness that Mohammed is God's apostle." Islam is based on strict monotheism in which there is little room for individual freedom. At least, that is the general western view from the middle of the nineteenth century continuing to today. But is that really the case?

PREDESTINATION AND FATALISM

Hard criticism of this strict monotheism and the resulting determinism and fatalism are by 1900 a matter of course among western religious scientists. The German theologian Friedrich Ulrich wrote in 1912: "... The Koran absolutely speaks of an all-powerful God."[86] And the American Samuel M. Zwemer: "Predestination is the cornerstone of the Muslim faith.... The practical effect is pure fatalism ... and has paralyzed all progress."[87] Zwemer wrote for the *Student Volunteer Movement for Foreign Missions*, an American missionary organization. The conclusion of the hefty study was that there is still a lot of Christian missionary work to do in the Arabic world. We encounter the same view among some esotericists. For instance, Rudolf Steiner had this opinion:

> We see, in the first place, that monotheism in a very strict form was instituted by Mohammed. It is a religion that looks up, as did Judaism, to a single Godhead encompassing the universe.... That is what goes forth from Arabia as a mighty impulse.... When we consider the form in which Mohammedanism made its appearance, we find, first and foremost, uncompromising monotheism, the one, all-powerful Godhead—a conception of

Divinity that is allied with fatalism. The destiny of man is predetermined; he must submit to his destiny, or at least recognize his subjection to it. This attitude is an integral part of the religious life.[88]

Nuance 1: Predestination and Freedom

In the colonial era already there were scientists who saw certain nuances in the predestination and fatalism of Islam. In 1908, the great German Islam scholar Ignaz Goldziher (1850-1921), who was of Hungarian descent, said about the Koran:

> There is no other doctrine [than free will] about which there are more contradictory passages in the Koran.... Over against many deterministic passages we can find an equal number of passages of the prophet [in which the free will is emphasized].[89]

Friedrich Ulrich states that the Koran (also) teaches individual responsibility[90] and refers to Sura 76: 28-31:

> We created them and made firm their make, and when We please We will bring in their place the likes of them by a change.
> Surely this is a reminder, so whoever pleases takes to his Lord a way. And you do not please except that Allah please, surely Allah is Knowing, Wise; He makes whom He pleases to enter into His mercy; and (as for) the unjust, He has prepared for them a painful chastisement.

Ulrich says about this Sura: "Here again, despite the seemingly deterministic content, human freedom of will and individual decision are maintained."[91] Ulrich says explicitly that fatalism cannot be found in the Koran; however, based on deterministic passages in the Koran a fatalistic view of life did develop. But this has more to do with the innate characteristics of oriental peoples. The doctrine of predestination of Mohammed in the Koran does have a fatalistic color but, at the same time, Mohammed opposes it. Determinism leads to fatalism if it is conceived mechanistically. With Mohammed that is not the case; it is a later development.[92] This has contributed to the spiritual rigidity of Mohammedan peoples. Ulrich also recognizes that it cannot be denied that in early eastern Christianity there was also a certain fatalistic tendency—despite a subsequent strong emphasis on the doctrine of freedom. We still see this also much later in Calvin (1509-1564) and his followers, who taught that Christ died only for the chosen ones.[93]

It seems as if Rudolf Steiner read Ulrich, because he also shaded his harsh statements about Islamic predestination and fatalism. In the Arabian Islam of Mohammed we can most certainly observe a freedom impulse. Not for nothing do all Muslims say with all their actions: *inshallah*—God willing. That saying presupposes human freedom, and this freedom has an uneasy relationship with the doctrine of *kismet* (predestination).[94] In this connection Steiner speaks very positively about Harun al-Rashid, the Abbasid Caliph in Baghdad. Steiner calls him a "highly cultured man" who was the center of a "spiritual culture of a very high order" in Baghdad. Baghdad was a center where Aristotelian philosophy, the natural sciences and the art of medicine flourished.[95]

There is most certainly an impulse toward individual freedom in Islam. In actual fact, every religion wrestles with the paradox of the will of God versus the free human will.[96] But, says Steiner, Islam is also influenced by retarding spiritual powers. In the original Arabian Islam there is still a strong impulse of the personality, but in the later Turkish Islam (starting with the Seljuks) more emphasis is placed on the Father God,[97] resulting in a stronger emphasis on predestination and fatalism. For that matter, we can observe the same development in Christianity. Steiner expresses it rather drastically: "If we disregard their words and consider their soul-spiritual content, many a Christian is actually a Turk."[98]

Predestination in Christianity

It is indeed quite possible to describe a comparable development toward predestination in Christianity. Often it is Augustine (354-430) who is held responsible for the emphasis on predestination (relative to the free will). That is not entirely justified. In the voluminous work of Augustine we can find differing statements about this. When he opposed the Manichaeans Augustine emphasized the free will. But when he fought against the Irish monk Pelagius (c.360-c.420) his emphasis was on predestination. Later theologians collected the statements in which Augustine emphasized predestination in his works.[99] This ended with Calvin (1509-1564). But in the middle of the ninth century it was still a development in process. In the middle of that century the so-called "first predestination battle" took place. The theologian Gottschalk of Orbais (c.808-c.867) even taught a "double predestination." He declared to the Synod of Bishops in 848:

> I, Gottschalk, believe, confess and avow before God the Father, by the Son in God and the Holy Spirit, assure and confirm before God and all

saints that there exists a double predestination, both of the chosen people for redemption and of the rejected people for damnation.[100]

This kind of view leaves little room for free will. Gottschalk was condemned as a heretic for his doctrine of double predestination. His opponents were not the least among Christian scholars: Hincmar of Reims (died 882) and Rabanus Maurus (died 856). Hincmar was archbishop of Reims, after Charlemagne the most powerful man in the West-Frankish realm, and Maurus was the most authoritative theologian of his time.[101] The battle therefore took place at high levels, and was decided in favor of free will. The first to tip the scales in favor of predestination was the great scholastic Anselm of Canterbury (1033-1109). In his book *De libertate arbitrii* (*About Freedom of Choice*) the question is: "When it is only God's grace that can free the sinner from his prison, how can the human being then have free will? The human being does indeed have free will, but he is too weak to orient his free will entirely on God. God must therefore show human beings the way. He does that by sending His Son who died for us weak human beings, and rose again: thus He reconciled the human being with God."[102] By himself the human being is quite powerless. The reconciliation doctrine of Anselm formed the basis for the later predestination doctrine of Calvin.

Nuance 2: From Polytheism to Monotheism

Mohammed developed his monotheism in reaction to the polytheism of the Arabian tribes. In Mohammed's time, around 600, every Arabian tribe on the Arabian peninsula had its own god. Generally these were a type of animistic divinities, i.e., the Arabs believed everything to be ensouled by gods. A god protected the tribe, their actions, the territory, the camels. Through rituals this protection could be invoked. The northern tribes around Palmyra venerated the god Abgal. The goddess Allat was the most important divinity of the tribe of Ad from Aram in the south of Arabia. This tribe is mentioned in the Koran where it reports that Allah says: "And (We destroyed) Ad and Samood" because "they were unjustly proud in the land" (Suras 29:38; 41:15).

In pre-Islamic times Allat was worshipped in the Kaaba in Mecca as one of the three principal divinities. The other two were al-Uzza and Manat. They are mentioned in the Koran (Sura 53-19). Allat was also worshipped by the Arabian Nabataeans in the famous city of Petra in Jordan, as was al-Uzza. Al-Uzza was a goddess whose name means "the most powerful"; she was a goddess of fertility.

The tribe of the Quraish called upon her, together with the god Hubal, when they went to war against the Muslims of Mohammed. Hubal was the principal god of the Quraish in the Kaaba. The Quraish were the protectors of the Kaaba. Hubal's wife was Manat, the goddess of fate.

There were 360 gods in the mythological pantheon of the Kaaba. One of these was Allah, the God of Abraham, the God therefore of those who believed in one sole God. Those who believed in one God in pre-Islamic Arabia were called the Hashemites.[103] Mohammed's father had the name Abdullah (from *Abd-Allah*, servant of Allah). Allah is therefore not an invention of Mohammed; he "existed" long before Mohammed. The only thing Mohammed did was to "promote" Allah to the sole God. But why did he do that? Mohammed saw how Arabian paganism with its many gods had degenerated and was ruining humanity. Sura 89 says:

> Have you not considered how your Lord dealt with Ad, (the people of) Aram, possessors of lofty buildings, the like of which were not created in the (other) cities; and (with) Samood, who hewed out the rocks in the valley, and (with) Firon, the lord of hosts, who committed inordinacy in the cities, so they made great mischief therein? (Sura 89: 6-12)

Mohammed wanted to do away with those pantheistic nature gods that brought ruin. This was the reason why he rejected the Christian doctrine of the Trinity. For in the triune God of Father, Son and Holy Spirit he saw the same danger of the multiplicity of gods. In the Christian view of Jesus as the Son of God, Mohammed sees two gods. The rejection of the Christian doctrine of the Trinity and the rejection of Jesus as the Son of God were decisive for the independent development of Islam. The Koran takes a very firm stand. In several Suras emphasis is placed on the fact that Allah did not "take to Himself a son" (19:35). Sura 4:171:

> O followers of the Book! do not exceed the limits in your religion, and do not speak (lies) against Allah, but (speak) the truth; the Messiah, Isa son of Maryam, is only an apostle of Allah and His Word which He communicated to Maryam and a spirit from Him; believe therefore in Allah and His apostles, and say not, Three. Desist, it is better for you; Allah is only one God; far be it from His glory that He should have a son, whatever is in the heavens and whatever is in the earth is His, and Allah is sufficient for a Protector.

Nuance 3: The Personal God

Thus Mohammed wanted to do away with the worship of nature gods. He substituted Allah for them. But Allah first had to be emancipated from the pantheon of the Kaaba and from nature. Mohammed brings this about. In the early Suras from Mecca, Mohammed speaks continually about *rabbika*, which is translated as "your Lord." Sura 96 was the first sura Mohammed received:

> Read in the name of your Lord Who created.
> He created man from a clot.
> Read and your Lord is Most Honorable,
> Who taught (to write) with the pen
> Taught man what he knew not. (Sura 96:1-5)

In this first Sura, the Creator appears as a personal God who can be experienced by every individual: your God! That is a huge change from the animistic gods of the Arabs. In later verses from Medina there continues to be mention of "your Lord" (Sura 99). God can only speak to me as an individual if God is one, and not many. The personal aspect of God is emphasized. According to Sufi master Dr. Mostafa Azmayesh, Mohammed never even mentioned Allah during the first five years of his revelations; he always spoke of "your Lord." He would have done this to prevent that Allah would have become the umpteenth god of the Kaaba. Only when he began his preaching did he start connecting "your Lord" with Allah. That was a name the Arabs would recognize. And later still, Mohammed made a connection between the personal Allah with the principal occupant of the Kaaba. The Kaaba then became the house of Allah:

> And when We assigned to Ibrahim the place of the House, saying: Do not associate with Me aught, and purify My House for those who make the circuit and stand to pray and bow and prostrate themselves. (Sura 22:26)

Later again, Mohammed's revelations continued their development toward a transcendent God:

> Follow what is revealed to you from your Lord; there is no god but He; and withdraw from the polytheists. (Sura 6:106)

Allah then became both a personal and a transcendent God. It is especially the Sufi tradition which orients itself to this personal, individual aspect of Allah. For if Allah is exclusively transcendent and unknowable, he cannot be experienced in the heart. Yet, many Islamic mystics bear witness to this.[104] The (western) representation of Allah as a sort of omnipotent despot does not match reality. For the pious Muslim, Allah is always near and can be invoked for help.[105] Sura 2 says:

> And when My servants ask you concerning Me, then surely I am very near; I answer the prayer of the suppliant when he calls on Me, so they should answer My call and believe in Me that they may walk in the right way. (Sura 2:186)

In this passage, Allah shows himself to be a merciful God who bestows forgiveness (Sura 14:41). He is a personal, loving God who speaks to people personally. That is a far cry from the old animistic divinities. The "emancipation" of Allah was decisive for the individualizing and freedom impulse of Islam. God is no longer tied to tribal gods, but to individuals. The revolution which Mohammed caused with this consists of breaking the tribal connection. Not tribes, but individuals know themselves connected with Allah. They connect with each other in a new community of Muslims, the *umma*.

Nuance 4: The 99 Names of God

The Koran begins as follows (Sura 1):

> In the name of Allah, Most Gracious, Most Merciful.
> Praise be to Allah, the Cherisher and Sustainer of the worlds;
> Most Gracious, Most Merciful;
> Master of the Day of Judgment.
> Thee do we worship, and Thine aid we seek.
> Show us the straight way,
> The way of those on whom Thou hast bestowed Thy Grace, those whose [portion] is not wrath, and who go not astray.

The first line is called the *bismillah*. Every Sura of the Koran (except Sura 9) begins with the *bismillah*: *"b-ismi-llāhi r-raḥmāni r-raḥīmi"*: "In the name of Allah, Most Gracious, Most Merciful."[106]

Here we experience a completely different tone than the revengeful, omnipotent, monotheistic God of predestination. Above all Allah is merciful. But he is much more: he has 99 names, and with the aid of prayer beads a Muslim will meditate on these 99 names. The names are (with the Suras in which they are mentioned):

1	Ar-Raḥmān	The Exceedingly Compassionate, The Exceedingly Beneficent, The Exceedingly Gracious	Beginning of every chapter except one, and in numerous other places. Name frequently used in surah 55, Ar-Rahman (57 times in surah)
2	Ar-Raḥīm	The Exceedingly Merciful	Beginning of every chapter except one, and in numerous other places (114 times in surah)
3	Al-Malik	The King	59:23, 20:114, 23:116
4	Al-Quddūs	The Holy, The Pure, The Perfect	59:23, 62:1
5	As-Salām	The Peace, The Source of Peace and Safety, The Savior	59:23
6	Al-Mu'min	The Guarantor, The Affirming	59:23
7	Al-Muhaymin	The Guardian	59:23
8	Al-'Azīz	The Almighty, The Invulnerable, The Honorable	3:6, 4:158, 9:40, 48:7, 59:23
9	Al-Jabbār	The Irresistible, The Compeller, The Lofty	59:23
10	Al-Mutakabbir	The Majestic, The Supreme	59:23
11	Al-Khāliq	The Creator	6:102, 13:16, 39:62, 40:62, 59:24
12	Al-Bāri'	The Evolver, The Fashioner, The Designer	59:24
13	Al-Muṣawwir	The Fashioner of Forms	59:24
14	Al-Ġaffār	The Repeatedly Forgiving	20:82, 38:66, 39:5, 40:42, 71:10
15	Al-Qahhār	The Subduer	12:39, 13:16, 14:48, 38:65, 39:4, 40:16
16	Al-Wahhāb	The Bestower	3:8, 38:9, 38:35
17	Ar-Razzāq	The Provider	51:58
18	Al-Fattāḥ	The Opener, The Victory Giver	34:26

19	Al-'Alīm	The All Knowing, The Omniscient	2:158, 3:92, 4:35, 24:41, 33:40
20	Al-Qābiḍ	The Restrainer, The Straightener	2:245
21	Al-Bāsiṭ	The Extender / Expander	2:245
22	Al-Khāfiḍ	The Abaser	56:3
23	Ar-Rāfi'	The Exalter	58:11, 6:83
24	Al-Mu'izz	The Giver of Honor	3:26
25	Al-Muḍill	The Giver of Dishonor	3:26
26	As-Samī'	The All Hearing	2:127, 2:256, 8:17, 49:1
27	Al-Baṣīr	The All Seeing	4:58, 17:1, 42:11, 42:27
28	Al-Ḥakam	The Judge, The Arbitrator	22:69
29	Al-'Adl	The Utterly Just	6:115
30	Al-Laṭīf	The Gentle, The Subtly Kind	6:103, 22:63, 31:16, 33:34
31	Al-Ḫabīr	The All Aware	6:18, 17:30, 49:13, 59:18
32	Al-Ḥalīm	The Forbearing, The Indulgent	2:235, 17:44, 22:59, 35:41
33	Al-'Aẓīm	The Magnificent	2:255, 42:4, 56:96
34	Al-Ġafūr	The Much-Forgiving	2:173, 8:69, 16:110, 41:32
35	Aš-Šakūr	The Grateful	35:30, 35:34, 42:23, 64:17
36	Al-'Alī	The Sublime	4:34, 31:30, 42:4, 42:51
37	Al-Kabīr	The Great	13:9, 22:62, 31:30
38	Al-Ḥafīẓ	The Preserver	11:57, 34:21, 42:6
39	Al-Muqīt	The Nourisher	4:85
40	Al-Ḥasīb	The Bringer of Judgment	4:6, 4:86, 33:39
41	Al-Ġalīl	The Majestic	55:27, 39:14, 7:143
42	Al-Karīm	The Bountiful, The Generous	27:40, 82:6
43	Ar-Raqīb	The Watchful	4:1, 5:117
44	Al-Muğīb	The Responsive, The Answer	11:61
45	Al-Wāsi'	The Vast, The All Embracing, The Omnipresent, The Boundless	2:268, 3:73, 5:54
46	Al-Ḥakīm	The Wise	31:27, 46:2, 57:1, 66:2
47	Al-Wadūd	The Loving	11:90, 85:14
48	Al-Mağīd	The All Glorious, The Majestic	11:73

49	Al-Bāʿiṯ	The Resurrecter	22:7
50	Aš-Šahīd	The Witness	4:166, 22:17, 41:53, 48:28
51	Al-Ḥaqq	The Truth, The Reality	6:62, 22:6, 23:116, 24:25
52	Al-Wakīl	The Trustee, The Dependable, The Advocate	3:173, 4:171, 28:28, 73:9
53	Al-Qawwī	The Strong	22:40, 22:74, 42:19, 57:25
54	Al-Matīn	The Firm, The Steadfast	51:58
55	Al-Walī	The Friend, Patron and Helper	4:45, 7:196, 42:28, 45:19
56	Al-Ḥamīd	The All Praiseworthy	14:8, 31:12, 31:26, 41:42
57	Al-Muḥṣī	The Accounter, The Numberer of All	72:28, 78:29, 82:10-12
58	Al-Mubdiʾ	The Originator, The Producer, The Initiator	10:34, 27:64, 29:19, 85:13
59	Al-Muʿīd	The Restorer, The Reinstater Who Brings Back All	10:34, 27:64, 29:19, 85:13
60	Al-Muḥyī	The Giver of Life	7:158, 15:23, 30:50, 57:2
61	Al-Mumīt	The Destroyer, The Bringer of Death	3:156, 7:158, 15:23, 57:2
62	Al-Ḥayy	The Living	2:255, 3:2, 25:58, 40:65
63	Al-Qayyūm	The Subsisting, The Guardian	2:255, 3:2, 20:111
64	Al-Wāǧid	The Perceiver, The Finder, The Unfailing	38:44
65	Al-Māǧid	The Illustrious, The Magnificent	85:15, 11:73,
66	Al-Wāḥid	The One, The Unique	2:163, 5:73, 9:31, 18:110
67	Al-ʾAḥad	The Unity, The Indivisible	112:1
68	Aṣ-Ṣamad	The Eternal, The Absolute, The Self-Sufficient	112:2
69	Al-Qādir	The Omnipotent, The All Able	6:65, 36:81, 46:33, 75:40
70	Al-Muqtadir	The Determiner, The Dominant	18:45, 54:42, 54:55
71	Al-Muqaddim	The Expediter, He Who Brings Forward	16:61, 17:34,
72	Al-Muʾakhkhir	The Delayer, He Who Puts Far Away	71:4
73	Al-ʾAwwal	The First, The Beginning-less	57:3
74	Al-ʾAḫir	The Last, The Endless	57:3
75	Aẓ-Ẓāhir	The Manifest, The Evident, The Outer	57:3
76	Al-Bāṭin	The Hidden, The Unmanifest, The Inner	57:3

77	Al-Wālī	The Patron, The Protecting Friend, The Friendly Lord	13:11, 22:7
78	Al-Mutaʻālī	The Supremely Exalted, The Most High	13:9
79	Al-Barr	The Good, The Beneficent	52:28
80	At-Tawwāb	The Ever Returning, Ever Relenting	2:128, 4:64, 49:12, 110:3
81	Al-Muntaqim	The Avenger	32:22, 43:41, 44:16
82	Al-ʻAfū	The Pardoner, The Effacer, The Forgiver	4:99, 4:149, 22:60
83	Ar-Ra'ūf	The Kind, The Pitying	3:30, 9:117, 57:9, 59:10
84	Mālik-ul-Mulk	The Owner of all Sovereignty	3:26
85	Dhū-l-Ġalāli wa-l-'ikrām	The Lord of Majesty and Generosity	55:27, 55:78
86	Al-Muqsiṭ	The Equitable, The Requiter	7:29, 3:18
87	Al-Ġāmiʻ	The Gatherer, The Unifier	3:9
88	Al-Ġanī	The Rich, The Independent	3:97, 39:7, 47:38, 57:24
89	Al-Muġnī	The Enricher, The Emancipator	9:28
90	Al-Māniʻ	The Withholder, The Shielder, The Defender	67:21
91	Aḍ-Ḍārr	The Distressor, The Harmer, The Afflictor	6:17
92	An-Nāfiʻ	The Propitious, The Benefactor, The Source of Good	30:37
93	An-Nūr	The Light	24:35
94	Al-Hādī	The Guide, The Way	22:54
95	Al-Badīʻ	The Incomparable, The Unattainable	2:117, 6:101
96	Al-Bāqī	The Immutable, The Infinite, The Everlasting	55:27
97	Al-Wāriṯ	The Heir, The Inheritor of All	15:23, 57:10
98	Ar-Rašīd	The Guide to the Right Path	2:256, 72:10
99	As-Sabur	The Timeless, The Patient	2:153, 3:200, 103:3

Chart Source: http://en.wikipedia.org/wiki/Names_of_God_in_the_Qur%27an#List_of_99_N.ames_of_God_as_found_in_the_Qur.27an

"There is no God but God!" Which God exactly?! God can be the Afflictor, the Omniscient and the Avenger. But he can also be the Merciful, the Forgiver and the Protector.

The Religion of the Seljuks

As was mentioned before, it was only with the invasion of the Seljuk Turks that Islam received the fatalistic character that is so strongly emphasized by westerners. How did that happen, and what is the special color the Seljuks gave to Islam? That is not an easy question to answer, because we know little of the Seljuks before their conversion to Islam around the year 1000. In the *Encyclopedia of Islam* there is no mention of the religion of the pre-Islamic Seljuks; neither is there in the *Encyclopedia Iranica*. So it will be a bit of guesswork.

Fortunately, we do have indications. To begin with, two of the four sons of Seljuk—the ruler who gave his name to this Turkic tribe—had Judaic-Christian names: Michael and Israel. But these could also have been Manichaean names. That would not be so strange, for the Seljuk Turks belonged to the Oghuz-Turkic tribes, which in turn formed part of the Gök Türk Empire that controlled all of Central Asia in the sixth and seventh centuries, from the Aral Sea to far into China. The Turkic Uighurs were also part of this empire. The Uighurs are still a Turkic minority of about ten million people in western China.

In 745 the (second) Gök Türk Empire split into an eastern and western part, of which the eastern part was an Uighur kingdom in which Christian Manichaeism was the state religion. The religion of the Oghuz Turks in the western part (today's Turkmenistan, Kazakhstan and Uzbekistan) seems to have been a mixture of Christian Manichaeism, Nestorianism, Zoroastrianism, and the old shaman religion of the supreme god Tengri (or Tanri or Tängri). *Tanri* is simply the old-Turkic work for the supreme God. We encounter this divinity in many Manichaean texts found along the Silk Road in these parts, such as the hymn to Tengri as the god of the dawn:

> **Hymn to the God of the Dawn**
> The God of the Dawn has come
> The God of the Dawn himself has come
> The God of the Dawn has come
> The God of the Dawn himself has come
> Arise, all you masters, all you brethren!
> We would praise the God of the Dawn!
> All-seeing Sun God, protect us!
> Visible Moon God, redeem us!
> God of the Dawn,
> Fragrant, sweet, bright, shining,

God of the Dawn! [five times]
God of the Dawn [five times][107]

The Sun and Moon God (kün ay tängri), who have to protect and save us, refer here to Jesus as the Messiah. In some Turkic-Manichaean texts Jesus-the-Messiah is called the Son of God, in old-Turkic: Tängri oyli. Also the Turkic rulers were viewed as divine and carried the name Tängri in their title. In this way the title of the Uighur king Bögü Khan (795-805) was *Tängridä Bulmis*. Another Manichaean king was addressed as *Tängrikän*, "the Divine." There are texts in which Tengri is invoked for the liberation of a poor sinner from his sins and evil. Tengri was the Manichaean *Father of Greatness*; in other words, the *Father of Greatness* was the original supreme Manichaean God as described in many Iranian (Sogdian) Manichaean texts.

When Manichaeism expanded from the West—from the Baghdad area, where the founder Mani (216-276) came from—more and more to the East, it gradually adopted the characteristics of the supreme god of the Turks, Tengri. This is possible because both in Manichaeism and in the old shaman religion of the Turks there existed a whole hierarchy of divinities before God worked on the earth and on humanity. The supreme god Tengri can remain completely transcendent and be present in nature phenomena at the same time, just as this is also the case in shamanistic nature religions.[108]

The Blue Heavenly God Tengri

Even today many Turks say Tengri or Tanri, not Allah, when they speak about God. Tengri is the most high, transcendent God of the spiritual (non-visible) heaven. Where this heaven is, no one is able to know. At the same time, Tengri was the creator of everything visible and invisible. But he was not alone—there was a whole pantheon of seventeen gods. First there was his wife Yer or Yer-Sub, a kind of Mother Earth. Another wife of Tengri was Umai, who gave the human being a spark of light. Her light radiated throughout creation. When the spark from Umai left the human being he died.

Earth, water, air, wind and fire were animistic gods, but in all of them Tengri was present—they were never worshipped without Tengri. The sun, moon and stars were also gods. A person of great prosperity was called a "person with a star." When nature gods were invoked in shamanistic rituals and prayers it was always at the same time an invocation of Tengri. Tengri could be experienced and was omnipresent. The entire creation hung on Tengri; his will was law. In the old-Turkic inscription on the tomb of the ruler Bilge Kagan (mid-eighth century) we read:

> All children of humanity are born as determined by Tengri and die as determined by Tengri.

Health and illness, prosperity and adversity—everything depended on Tengri. The Turkic ruler governed in the name of Tengri, as a son of Tengri. Wisdom was given him, or withheld from him, by Tengri. It is Tengri who summoned the ruler and the warriors to combat, and he assured them of success if they prayed sufficiently to him. The dreaded (Turkic) leader of the Mongols, Genghis Khan, dedicated his successes to Tengri or to *Munkh Huh Tenger* (the eternally blue heaven).[109]

Are we seeing here the precursor of the (supposed) characteristics of predestination and fatalism of Seljuk Islam?

AL-GHAZALI

Around the year 1000 Seljuk, and with him the entire tribe of Seljuks, converted to Islam. At the same time the triumphal expansion of the Seljuks began. Under Seljuk's sons Michael (called Tugrul Beg) and Chagri Beg, Khorasan was conquered in 1034, the area that was subdued by Arabic Islam—the tribe of the Abbasids—in 651. And in 900 the Iranian Samanids had taken power there; they organized the region after the example of the Islamic Abbasids. This was the (orthodox) Sunni Islam. When in 1034 the Seljuks invaded the area a process of assimilation took place which was guided in an intellectual-theological sense by one of the greatest Islamic thinkers, Al-Ghazali (1058-1111). Al-Ghazali came from the city of Kus in Khorasan. He was born not long after the Seljuks had conquered Khorasan and also not long after the Turks had exchanged Tengri for Allah. In this connection the *Encyclopaedia of Islam* says about Al-Ghazali:

> It was the special task of Al-Ghazali—a man whose entire career took place during the peaceful decades of Seljuk power—to develop a theoretical basis for this relationship and collaboration between caliph and sultan.[110]

For Seljuk Islam, therefore, we have to study Al-Ghazali. Who was he, and what did he teach? Al-Ghazali was a Persian (Iranian) philosopher belonging to the Samanids. He was also a Sufi, which explains a lot, because the path of the Islamic mystics was different from that of the Islamic philosophers. In the

Islamic world he is called *Hujjat al-Islam*, meaning "proof of Islam," and among the Sunnites he is considered the greatest teacher after Mohammed. In 1085 he joined the court of Sultan Malik Shah in Baghdad. In Baghdad and other cities, Sultan Malik founded institutes for religious studies, the so-called *Nizamiyyah*. In 1092 Al-Ghazali was appointed there as a teacher of law. He was a popular and charismatic teacher with many students. But he was also a critical person and discovered that this work did not satisfy him. He made an about-face and began an eleven-year journey through the Muslim world and through his own inner being. Al-Ghazali became a Sufi! He described the process of this turnaround in a little book entitled *Deliverance from Error*. Here Al-Ghazali stated why he had turned away from philosophy and devoted himself to mysticism:

> You have asked me, O brother in the faith, to expound the aim and the mysteries of religious sciences, the boundaries and depths of theological doctrines. You wish to know my experiences while disentangling truth lost in the medley of sects and divergencies of thought, and how I have dared to climb from the low levels of traditional belief to the topmost summit of assurance. You desire to learn what I have borrowed, first of all from scholastic theology; and secondly from the method of the Ta'limites, who, in seeking truth, rest upon the authority of a leader; and why, thirdly, I have been led to reject philosophic systems; and finally, what I have accepted of the doctrine of the Sufis, and the sum total of truth which I have gathered in studying every variety of opinion. You ask me why, after resigning at Baghdad a teaching post which attracted a number of hearers, I have, long afterward, accepted a similar one at Nishapur. Convinced as I am of the sincerity which prompts your inquiries, I proceed to answer them, invoking the help and protection of God.[111]

In several of his books Al-Ghazali showed that it is not possible to come near to God through the intellect. With the aid of the methods and arguments of philosophy he unmasked those same methods and arguments. He especially targeted Ibn Sina, known in the West as the philosopher Avicenna (980-1037) who came from the same general area as Al-Ghazali. Together with Averroes (1126-1198) in Spain, Avicenna was in the West one of the best-known Islamic philosophers in the Middle Ages.

Al-Ghazali is often connected with "the closing of the gates of *ijtihad*" in the tenth century. *Ijtihad* means free and independent research (see also parts 2 and 3 in this book). Al-Ghazali's criticism of philosophy was supposed to be the reason for the "closing of the gates." But Al-Ghazali cannot be blamed for "the closing of the gates of *ijtihad*." Even ignoring the historical impossibility (he died in 1111), in his book *Ihya'ul ulum al-din* (*Revival of the Religious Sciences*) he defended *ijtihad* against the authority of the imam. In this book Al-Ghazali listed eight conditions which "the search for truth as part of religion" had to satisfy. The third condition which the seeker for truth has to satisfy is:

> ... should have the ability and right to form an opinion of his own (*mujtahid*), and should be one who can give decisions on his own responsibility without being bound to the opinions of the *imam*.[112]

Al-Ghazali is therefore not unconditionally opposed to independent research and freely formed opinions. While it is true that the quotation refers to Islamic law, it can also be applied to philosophy, because the criticism of Al-Ghazali is not on philosophy as such, but on the way it is practiced. Only when philosophy is practiced without reference to theology and mysticism Al-Ghazali draws the line. In *Tahafut al-Falasifa* he presents his arguments for this position. Moreover, "the gates of ijtihad" may have been closed in the tenth century, but this certainly did not result in the death of philosophy in the Muslim world. See for this Christine Gruwez's review of Islamic philosophy in part 3 of this book.

Tahafut al-Falasifa

In twenty chapters Al-Ghazali deals with the views, arguments and methods with which philosophers discourse on the eternity of God, His being and nature, His manner of creating, His attributes and the question of whether God knows His own creation. It is a discourse about the providence of God, the question of whether the creation has its own dynamics irrespective of God (the view of atheists) and whether God is independent of natural law and can change this law to His liking (for instance in miracles).

It is also about the human being: is the soul pre-existent and non-physical, or does it only come into existence with the body, as Avicenna contends (as did Thomas Aquinas in western scholasticism)? And where does the soul go after death? Is the body resurrected at the end of time, and does *metempsychosis* (reincarnation) exist? According to Al-Ghazali that is not the case. In brief, the entire philosophical-theological scholastic discussion is there.

Regularly Al-Ghazali emphasizes that for him the point is not whether he agrees or disagrees with the views of the philosophers, but that he wants to demonstrate the flaws in their argumentation. Two elements come to the fore again and again: (1) the philosophers interpret the Koran metaphorically and allegorically, and (2) human reason is insufficient in subjects like this. For instance, how can human reason know if the expectation of the end of time, as described in the Koran, was meant as an allegory? Why would Allah be incapable of resurrecting the human body at the end of time? In addition, the descriptions in the Koran of the end of time are so clear that there is no room for interpretation. For this reason, it is necessary to accept what the texts are literally saying, and not to pull things out of context.[113] It is not reason but religion which teaches us that the body shall be resurrected. God's ways are inscrutable and incomprehensible to human beings:

> Nay, the treasure house of things to which divine power extends includes mysterious and wonderful things which have not been discovered by man.... And then he will come to know how his own knowledge had failed to encompass the mysterious effects of Omnipotence.

Al-Ghazali does not spare the philosophers. They deviate from Islam (chapter 3); philosophical discussions about God merely lead to idle speculation (chapter 3). With reason and imagination we cannot find God (chapter 4); philosophical reasoning can only lead to denials (chapter 8) and even has to conclude that God is dead:

> This is what necessarily follows from your [the philosophers'] basic thought. There is no difference between you and one who would say: (a) that everyone who has no volitional action, no power, no choice, and who does not hear and see, is dead; and (b) that he who does not know what is other than himself is dead.[114]

And that is precisely what the philosophers say about God: that He has no will of His own, that the creation proceeds from Him as a necessity, and that He knows only Himself (chapter 20). The final outcome is that they destroy "all divine Glory" (chapter 3).

The Alchemy of Happiness

No, all these intellectual disputations about God and his inimitable works will never lead to "true" knowledge of God. But then, what to do? How can we be saved from this error? Through Sufism, says Al-Ghazali in *Kīmyāyé Sa'ādat* (*The Alchemy of Happiness*), a Persian summary of *Ihya*. In this book Al-Ghazali explains his mystical path based on the mystical idea that self-knowledge leads to God-knowledge because the human being alone was created in the image of God. Through self-exploration (are you oriented on yourself or on God?), through meditation and contemplation of (the names of) God, the Koran and the prophets, and by abstinence and asceticism, the Sufi approaches God. Thus says *Kīmyāyé Sa'ādat*. But the effect of the love between God and the mystic does have to be visible in outer signs. Al-Ghazali lists seven signs:

1. One is no longer afraid of death, for only after death will we truly behold God;
2. One will sacrifice one's will to God; one surrenders to God (the literal meaning of the word Islam);
3. Remembering God will be a living impulse in the heart, for what one loves is always a living presence in one's heart;
4. The will to love the Koran, for this is the word of God. But also the love of Mohammed and, in fact, all human beings (compare Christian *charity*);
5. The Sufi will long for seclusion so as to be able to live devotedly and in community with his Friend (Allah);
6. Worship will become easier and easier—it becomes habit;
7. The loved ones of God will love all who obey God, and will hate those who disobey God.[115]

That is a beautiful program...for a mystic! But if the outer signs are not based on inner life, it can all too easily become orthodoxy. That is the way it goes in religions. We can see parallels in Judaism and Christianity. Protestant mysticism from the seventeenth century turned into ultra-orthodoxy, and orthodox Judaism has its roots in Hassidism of the seventeenth and eighteenth centuries.

Conclusion

Al-Ghazali (1058-1111) lived around the same time as Bernard de Clairvaux (1090-1153) in France. Bernard is considered the inaugurator of the Christian mysticism of the Middle Ages. He took a strong stand against the upcoming scholasticism of Abelard (1079-1142), who said that one can discover all mysteries of the faith with the intellect. Bernard, however, said that this can only be done through mysticism.[116] He wrote the following about Abelard in a letter to the pope:

We have a new theologian here in France, a former master in the liberal arts who in his youth played around in rhetoric but now proclaims foolishness concerning the Holy Scriptures.... He pretends to know everything that is above in the heavens and here below on earth; except for the words "I don't know" he knows everything. He lifts his mouth up to the heavens and there he investigates the sublimity of God; upon his return he relates to us unspeakable things in words that are incompatible with human language. As he is ready to bare the reason of absolutely everything, he also pretends to be able to explain that which transcends reason, even though this goes against reason itself, and also against faith.[117]

Al-Ghazali could have said it. Al-Ghazali thus has his Christian counterpart in Bernard de Clairvaux. But whereas Al-Ghazali "won" in Islam, Bernard "lost" in Christianity. In western Christianity the future went to scholasticism and intellectualism, not least because of Averroes (see also part 3). All of this led to the fact that in Islam "submission" to Allah—taken out of its mystical context—became dominant, while in the West the intellect became dominant. In the words of the Moroccan author Abkader Chrifi: "With us Allah comes first, then the community, then the family, and only then comes the 'I.'" But did Mohammed intend it that way?

Chapter 4

Jesus in Islam

In the Koran and in the *hadith*[*] Isa (Jesus) plays a very important role. That is not so immediately evident to the average Muslim, let alone for Christians. In the ninth century Christian eyewitnesses spoke about Islam as a Christian heresy. How important is Isa, and how does the Islamic Isa relate to the Christian Jesus?

Isa in the Koran

Isa is frequently mentioned in the Koran. After Abraham he is the most important prophet. In a certain sense, Isa is even the most important apostle of Allah, because he is the Word and Spirit of Allah (Sura 4:171):

> ... The Messiah, Isa son of Maryam, is only an apostle of Allah and His Word which He communicated to Maryam and a spirit from Him.

That is said about no other prophet. The saying that Isa is the Word of God and a Spirit from Him is not the only thing that makes Isa unique in the Koran. For Isa was also born from a virgin. This is very beautifully described in Sura *Maryam* (Sura 19). When Mary is in seclusion, an angel appeared to her:

> We sent to her Our spirit, and there appeared to her a well-made man. She said: Surely I fly for refuge from you to the Beneficent God, if you are one guarding (against evil). He said: I am only a messenger of your Lord: That

---

[*] Translator's note: In Islamic terminology, *hadith* refers to reports of statements or actions of Mohammed, or of his tacit approval or criticism of something said or done in his presence.... The overwhelming majority of Muslims consider *hadith* to be essential supplements to and clarifications of the Koran, Islam's holy book, as well as in clarifying issues pertaining to Islamic jurisprudence. (Source: Wikipedia)

I will give you a pure boy. She said: When shall I have a boy and no mortal has yet touched me, nor have I been unchaste? He said: Even so; your Lord says: It is easy to Me: and that We may make him a sign to men and a mercy from Us, and it is a matter which has been decreed. So she conceived him; then withdrew herself with him to a remote place. (Sura 19:17-22)

The Koran also teaches the virgin birth! And there is more. It is Isa who returns at the end of time to do battle against the Antichrist. We read in Sura 4:159:

And there is not one of the followers of the Book but most certainly believes in this before his death, and on the day of resurrection he (Isa) shall be a witness against them.

This verse does not directly mention Isa, but tradition teaches that it refers to him; but this does not have everyone's full agreement.[118] Isa will return at the Last Judgment and will redeem the earth from evil.[119] In this view, Sura 4:159 is usually connected with Sura 43:61 where Isa is called "knowledge of the hour."[120] At any rate, this combination has led to many *hadith* about the return of Isa. Generally speaking the story is as follows:

The Antichrist will counter the teaching of Isa by proclaiming that Isa is above God and that because of his crucifixion the world was redeemed. The Antichrist will establish a kingdom in Jerusalem, which will be destroyed by Isa the Messiah. Isa shall appear with a spear in his hand to the east of the Sea of Galilee. With the spear he will kill the Antichrist. Isa will then go to Jerusalem at the time of morning prayer and will, together with the rest of the Muslims, pray on the temple square in conformity with Islamic law. Next he will break all crosses and destroy the synagogues and churches in the city. Isa will then reign for forty days or forty years on earth. When he dies he will be buried in Medina.[121]

This is then elaborated in the *hadith* in many eschatological stories. Some of these follow below. The best known one is by Bukhari (810-890):

By Him in whose hand my soul is, surely the son of Mary will soon descend among us as a just ruler; he will break the Cross and kill the pigs and there will be no Jizya [tax imposed on non-Muslims]. Money will be in abundance so that nobody will accept it, and a single prostration to Allah (in prayer) will be better than the whole world and whatever is in it.[122]

Another version is from the hand of Zamakhshari (1075-1144):

> Jesus (on him be peace) will descend on a narrow pass in the holy land Afiq wearing two light yellow garments, the hair of his head lank, in his hand a lance with which he will kill the Antichrist. Then he will go to Jerusalem when the people are at dawn prayer led by the imam. The imam will move back, but Jesus will give him precedence and pray behind him in accordance with the *sharia* of Muhammad (the peace and blessings of God be upon him). Then he will kill the pigs, break the cross, demolish oratories and churches and kill Christians except those who believe in him.[123]

The fact that Isa will give precedence to the imam and will destroy the symbols of Christianity and Judaism means that Isa has become a Muslim.[124]

The Sufi Ibn Kathir (1301-1373) relates:

> God will send the Messiah, Son of Mary, and he will descend at the white minaret on the eastern side of Damascus wearing garments lightly colored with saffron and placing his hands on the wings of the angels. Then he will pursue him [the Antichrist] and overtake him and kill him by the eastern gate of Lod.[125]

Al-Tabari (839-922) relates a *hadith* about the nocturnal journey of Mohammed:

> On the night of the night journey, I met Abraham, Moses and Jesus. They were conferring with each other concerning the Hour. They submitted the matter to Abraham, and Abraham said: "I have no knowledge of it." So they submitted the matter to Moses, and Moses said: "I have no knowledge of it." So they submitted the matter to Jesus. He said: "Regarding the arising of the Hour, no one has knowledge of it apart from God. But my Lord has confided in me everything about it except the time of its occurrence. He has confided in me that the Antichrist will come out, and that He will cause me to alight to meet him.... When he sees me God will destroy him.[126]

Another story from Tabari:

> The messenger of God (the peace and blessings of God be upon him!) said: "The principal sign will be the Antichrist, the descent of Jesus, a fire which will come from the depths of Aden and drive mankind to the gathering place where they will be told all that they said [the judgment]....

Jesus and the Muslims will be on the Mount Sinai and God (majestic is His majesty) will reveal to Jesus: "Keep my servants on the mountain and in proximity to Aelia (Jerusalem). Jesus shall lift his head to the heavens and the Muslims shall believe."[127]

Death on the Cross?

Two important points of doctrine are shared by Christianity and Islam regarding Jesus: the virgin birth and the return at the end of time. But the third doctrine, one could say in between these two, namely the manner in which Jesus died, has been the subject of furious fights through the centuries. Sura 4:156-158 says:

> And for their unbelief and for their having uttered against Maryam a grievous calumny. And their saying: Surely we have killed the Messiah, Isa son of Maryam, the apostle of Allah; and they did not kill him nor did they crucify him, but it appeared to them so (like Isa) and most surely those who differ therein are only in a doubt about it; they have no knowledge respecting it, but only follow a conjecture, and they killed him not for sure. Nay! Allah took him up to Himself; and Allah is Mighty, Wise.

And Sura 3:55:

> ... Allah said: O Isa, I am going to terminate the period of your stay (on earth) and cause you to ascend unto Me and purify you of those who disbelieve....

The Old Testament reports that there were other prophets who ascended to God without having died, including the enigmatic Enoch:

> Enoch walked with God; then he was no more, because God took him away. (Gen 5:24)

In the apocryphal Enoch books it is related that Enoch was subsequently elevated to the archangel Metatron.[128]
According to the New Testament, Jesus' end was similar at the Ascension:

> After he said this, he was taken up before their very eyes, and a cloud hid him from their sight. (Acts 1:9)

In the Acts of the Apostles of the New Testament the Ascension takes place forty days after Jesus' resurrection. And although in the Koran it is not clear whether Jesus had then died (on the cross), it is certain that also in the Koran Isa ascended into heaven. The Ascension of Jesus in the New Testament is based on the older Jewish ascensions of Enoch and Isaiah. As to Jesus, the early Christians interpreted this in their own way. And thus it seems as if Mohammed also interpreted Jewish and Christian ascensions in his own way. After all, Isa had been begotten with Mary by the spirit of Allah, and could therefore just as easily be taken up by Allah. Thus we see in the Koran:

1. Isa as the Word and the Spirit;
2. The virgin birth;
3. Isa as an extraordinary prophet; and
4. The Ascension.

What is lacking are the cross and the Resurrection. And that is precisely the crux of the matter.

Problems

But now it becomes more complicated. For there are also arguments that could lead one to believe that things happened differently. First, there is the problem of Sura 4:156-158, which says that the Jews had the impression that Jesus had died on the cross, whereas this was not the case. It is the only verse in the entire Koran in which the death on the cross is so emphatically denied. Professor Nasr Abu Zayd of the *Universiteit voor Humanistiek* in Utrecht points out that, if the death on the cross and the resurrection are such defining differences between Christianity and Islam, it is strange that the death on the cross is only mentioned once in the Koran, especially since it occurs in a passage about Jews, not Christians. According to Nasr, the Koran says here that the *Jews* thought that they had crucified Jesus, whereas something like this lies of course exclusively in the hands of Allah: "it was suggested to them."[129] The verse does not say that Jesus was not crucified; it merely says that the Jews thought that *they* had crucified him. It is a possibility.

The second problem is in the phrase "it was suggested to them." Another translation reads: "... but a semblance was made to them."[130] John Damascene (676-749), one of the great Oriental church fathers of Arab descent, was one of the first to make a study of the Koran. He wrote:

> The Jews ... wanted to crucify him and after they arrested him they crucified his shadow, but Christ himself, they say, was not crucified, nor did he die; For God took him up to himself into heaven because He loved him.[131]

With this interpretation of Sura 4:157, John suggests that Islam is a sort of Gnostic-Christian sect. Mohammed then would have had a Docetic* view of Christ, namely that Jesus (the shadow) did indeed die on the cross, but not Christ. Irrespective of the question of whether this is correct, it is at any rate interesting that John Damascene viewed Islam as a Christian sect. Many Muslims believe that it was Judas Iscariot who died on the cross in lieu of Jesus. This is stated in the apocryphal *Gospel of Barnabas*.

The third problem has to do with the history of the Koran. Tradition says that the Koran was revealed to Mohammed in its entirety and without modifications. Reality is of course more complicated because the Koran also has a history of development; at least, this is the view of some scientists, who are considered as belonging to the so-called "revisionist" school (see also chapter 2). According to the revisionists, such as the German Islam scholar Luxenberg (a pseudonym), the Koran contains passages that had already circulated in Yemen before Mohammed; other texts seem to have been borrowed from the Christian liturgy of the Syrian Church. Other passages again are modeled on apocryphal Christian stories, which can actually be demonstrated (see *Apocryphal Stories* hereafter). According to Luxenberg most of these stories were in Aramaic, the translation of which into Arabic presents many problems. Both are Semitic languages in which, in Mohammed's time, vowels were not written. These were added later, and this may have led to errors. One of the translation problems relates to the death on the cross. Luxenberg sees such a translation problem in Sura 72:19. The translation we have been quoting reads:

---

* Translator's note: *Docetism* is defined narrowly as "the doctrine according to which the phenomenon of Christ, his historical and bodily existence, and thus above all the human form of Jesus, was altogether mere semblance without any true reality." Broadly it is taken as the belief that Jesus only seemed to be human, and that his physical body was a phantasm. (Source: Wikipedia)

> And that when the servant of Allah stood up calling upon Him, they well-nigh crowded him (to death).

That is incomprehensible, also in the context of the passage. Luxenberg therefore went back to the Aramaic, especially for the words "stands forth." With the help of Aramaic, he then translated the passage as follows:

> ... When the servant of Allah *arose* and continued calling upon Him, they [the people] almost worshipped him [as God].[132]

The word *qaam* means "he stands forth [or stood up]" both in Aramaic and in Arabic; however, it can also mean "he rose from death."[133] And if we then add to this the possibility that, in the view of the revisionists, the phrase "servant of Allah" might not refer to Mohammed but to Jesus (see chapter 2), it turns into a completely different sentence in which, mark you, the resurrection is mentioned. If this verse appeared in the early Koran in the way suggested by Luxenberg, our little list may be expanded to the following:

1. Isa as the Word and the Spirit;
2. The virgin birth;
3. Isa as an extraordinary prophet;
4. (Death and) resurrection; and
5. The Ascension.

The only difference—although crucial—that then remains with Oriental Christianity is the fact that Mohammed did not teach that Jesus died on the cross. But he did teach that Jesus rose again after his death and ascended into heaven. By the way, the resurrection of Jesus is mentioned literally in the Koran, in Sura 19. There the baby Jesus speaks to the bystanders:

> And peace on me on the day I was born, and on the day I die, and on the day I am raised to life. (Sura 19:33)

According to Koran exegetists, this verse refers to the resurrection at the end of time. For, Isa has been taken up into heaven, will return at some time and rule for forty years to defeat the Antichrist, after which he will die in order to rise again at the end of time to judge humanity (see the *hadith* above).[134]

There is a remarkable *hadith* that relates the following:

> Al-Uris saw in his sleep Christ Jesus, Son of Mary, who seemed to turn his face toward him from heaven. Al-Uris asked him: "Did the crucifixion really happen?" Jesus said: "Yes, the crucifixion really happened." Al-Uris then related his dream to an interpreter who said: "The man who saw this dream shall be crucified. For Jesus is infallible and can speak only the truth, yet the crucifixion he spoke of cannot refer to his own, because the glorious Quran specifically states that Jesus was not crucified or killed. Accordingly, this must refer to the dreamer, and it is he who shall be crucified." The matter turned out as the interpreter said.[135]

According to this *hadith*, Jesus did speak the truth, but because it is not in the Koran, it cannot be *the* truth. Be this as it may, the story shows that also regarding the death on the cross (or not) Islam comes close to traditional Christian doctrine. Tradition and Islamic orthodoxy hold that it is crystal clear that Jesus did not die on the cross, but there is sufficient reason to presume that he rose again after his death (which did not happen on the cross).

Christianity in Mecca

From Mohammed's biography we know that around 605—Mohammed was then 35 years old—the Kaaba was destroyed. The reconstruction of the Kaaba was directed by a "*Rum*" with the name of Baaqum (chapter 8). A *Rum* is a Roman, in other words, a Byzantine which, in turn, means a Christian. The Kaaba reconstructed by a Christian!? Even more astounding are the reports that at one time there were images of Jesus and Mary in the Kaaba. Al-Azriqi (died 834) wrote in his *Akhbar Makka al-Musharrafa* (Chronicle of the City of Mecca):

> On the day when Mohammed entered Mecca in triumph, he ordered the destruction of all idols and religious images. However, when he saw a picture of the Virgin Mary and the child Jesus in the Kaaba, he reverently covered it with his cloak. He commanded that while all other images should be destroyed, the image of the Madonna with her Child should be considered sacred.[136]

Evidently, Christians also had a place in the Kaaba in pre-Islamic times. The last word has not been said about Christianity on the Arabian peninsula and in

Mecca in Mohammed's time. However, one thing is certain: Mohammed was acquainted with a variety of forms of Christianity that are not well-known in the West. For instance, we can see an influence of Manichaeism in the eschatology of Islam, and the Koran seems to follow the discussions on the nature of Jesus Christ under the Nestorians and Monophysites.

The Nestorian Christians held that Jesus was in the first instance human, and in the course of his life grew toward divine status because his will became more and more one with the will of God. Not until his death was he glorified by God and taken up to sit at His right hand. The Monophysites believed that the sequence was the other way around: Jesus was God from birth. In the Koran we find stories of the youth of Isa in which he already performs miracles (see below). On the other hand, the Koran specifically denies that Isa is the Son of God.

Mohammed's fifth wife, Mariya, was a Monophysite Christian from Ethiopia. And when Mohammed was bewildered after his first revelations and sought help, his first wife, Khadijah, took him to her uncle Waraqah, who well knew what to say about these revelations:

> When I came to Khadijah I narrated to her what I had seen, and she said: "Be of good cheer and comfort thyself! I swear by him in whose hand the life of Khadijah is, that I hope that thou wilt be the prophet of this nation!" Then she rose, collected her garments around her and departed to Waraqah. She described to him what the apostle of Allah had seen and heard, and Waraqah exclaimed: "Holy! Holy! I swear by him in whose hand the life of Waraqah is, that the law of Moses has been bestowed on him and he is the prophet of this nation! Tell him to stand firm." Khadijah then returned to the apostle of Allah and informed him of what Waraqah had said.

This is plainly related in the biography of Mohammed, chapter 10.[137]

Apocryphal Stories

The Koran has stories about Isa which are derived from apocryphal Christian scripture. First of all, Marjam is described in the Koran as a temple priestess. Her father is called Imraan and his wife "wife of Imraan." They are unable to have children and therefore beseech God. God hears their prayer and the wife of Imraan becomes pregnant. In thankfulness she dedicates the child to the temple where it is placed in the care of old Zakariya (Zachariah). Then it says:

> ... and gave her into the charge of Zakariya; whenever Zakariya entered the sanctuary to (see) her, he found with her food. He said: O Maryam! whence comes this to you? She said: It is from Allah. Surely Allah gives to whom He pleases without measure. There did Zakariya pray to his Lord; he said: My Lord! grant me from Thee good offspring; surely Thou art the Hearer of prayer. Then the angels called to him as he stood praying in the sanctuary: That Allah gives you the good news of Yahya verifying a Word from Allah, and honorable and chaste and a prophet from among the good ones. He said: My Lord! when shall there be a son (born) to me, and old age has already come upon me, and my wife is barren? He said: Even thus does Allah what He pleases. He said: My Lord! appoint a sign for me. Said He: Your sign is that you should not speak to men for three days except by signs; and remember your Lord much and glorify Him in the evening and the morning. And when the angels said: O Maryam! surely Allah has chosen you and purified you and chosen you above the women of the world. O Maryam! keep to obedience to your Lord and humble yourself, and bow down with those who bow. This is of the announcements relating to the unseen which We reveal to you; and you were not with them when they cast their pens (to decide) which of them should have Maryam in his charge, and you were not with them when they contended one with another. (Sura 3: 37-44)

Who was finally chosen in this lottery to have charge of Mary is not related in the Koran. We do find this in the apocryphal Christian *Gospel of James*, which has almost the same story but with the addition that Joseph was the one chosen to have charge of Mary. The *Arabic Infancy Gospel of the Savior* tells of the miracles the child Jesus was able to perform. Among other things, he was able to bring birds made of clay to life. The same story appears in the *Infancy Gospel of Thomas*. Here Thomas relates:

> Then, taking soft clay from the mud, he formed twelve sparrows. It was the Sabbath when he did these things, and many children were with him. And a certain Jew, seeing the boy Jesus with the other children doing these things, went to his father Joseph and falsely accused the boy Jesus, saying that on the Sabbath he made clay, which is not lawful, and fashioned twelve sparrows. And Joseph came and rebuked him, saying: "Why are you doing these things on the Sabbath?" But Jesus, clapping his hands, commanded the birds with a shout in front of everyone and

said: "Go, take flight, and remember me, living ones." And the sparrows, taking flight, went away squawking. When the Pharisee saw this he was amazed and reported it to all his friends.[138]

We find a similar story in the Koran:

> And He will teach him the Book and the wisdom and the Tavrat and the Injeel. And (make him) an apostle to the children of Israel: That I have come to you with a sign from your Lord, that I determine for you out of dust like the form of a bird, then I breathe into it and it becomes a bird with Allah's permission. (Sura 3:48-49)

In the West, we don't know these kinds of stories on the youth of Jesus any more, but in the Muslim world they are well known because they are in the Koran.

Mohammed the Mystic

In his youth, Mohammed traveled with the trading caravans of his uncle Abutalib to Basra, south of Damascus in Syria. With some regularity he encountered Bahira there, one of the greatest Christian monks:

> When the caravan halted by the city of Basra, on the border of Shaam, one of the greatest Christian monks came to him. The name of the monk was Bahira. He walked through the caravan until he had reached the prophet; he took him by the arm and said: "This is the lord of the inhabitants of the world, the apostle of the Lord of all inhabitants of the world. Allah, the Sublime, will send him in His mercy for all inhabitants of the world." The people asked him: "How do you know this?" He said: "At your arrival from Aqaba, every rock and tree kneeled down, and they only do that for a prophet. I recognize him by the sign on his shoulder that resembles an apple, and we have read about him in our books."[139]

Bahira was a Christian monk in the tradition of the desert monks, such as Simeon the Stylite in Syria and Saint Anthony in Egypt. Bahira was an honorific for these holy men. Just like Moses and Jesus they frequently withdrew into the solitude of the desert to practice asceticism, but also to come into contact with the divine. In this way Mohammed learned the ascetic practices of Bahira in Syria. Just as Bahira did, Mohammed often withdrew into the cave of Hira to practice asceticism and to hear the voice of Allah via Jibreel (Gabriel). Some Sufis view themselves in the tradition of such ascetic monks. Before his move to Medina Mohammed was a mystic. Thus Mohammed made a journey into heaven, just like so many in the Jewish esoteric tradition and Christian mystical tradition of the desert fathers.[140] Indeed, the Sufis orient themselves much more strongly on Isa than on Mohammed. Sufis travel the path of Jesus, the *Imitatio Christi*.[141] Isa is the prototype of a Sufi:

> Jesus constantly traveled through the country, without ever staying in a house or village. His clothes consisted of a rough pilous or camelhair cloak and two woven shirts. In his hand he carried a staff. Always when night had fallen his lamp was the moonlight, his shadow the blackness of the night, his bed the earth, his pillow a stone and his food the plants of the fields. From time to time he did not eat for days. In times of difficulties and concern he was happy, and in times of wellbeing he was sad.[142]

Thus said Abu Rifa'a al-Fasawi (died 902). There are hundreds of stories like this about the itinerant ascetic and wise Isa, or Christ; for "Jesus" and "Christ" are used as interchangeable names (see below).

THE CHRIST EXPERIENCE OF MOHAMMED

The biography of Mohammed relates the story of his journey into heaven. In the Dome of the Rock in Jerusalem is shown what is supposed to be the footprint of Mohammed at the moment when he ascended into heaven on his heavenly steed Buraaq. In brief, the heavenly journey went as follows. Mohammed was accompanied by Jibreel (Gabriel). In the first heaven he met Adam, in the second heaven he met Mohammed Yahiah (John the Baptist) and Isa, in the third heaven Yusuf (Joseph, one of the twelve sons of Jacob). In the fourth heaven he met Harun ibn Imraan (Aaron), in the sixth heaven Musa ibn Imraan (Moses) and in the seventh heaven Ibrahim (Abraham). Finally, Mohammed rose up past the seventh heaven, the "lotus tree of the final destination" and stood "at two bow-lengths distance" facing the countenance of God Himself. God commanded Mohammed and his people to say fifty prayers each twenty-four hours. On the way back, Moses asked what God had ordered Mohammed to do. The latter answered: fifty prayers a day. Moses thought that was too much. He advised Mohammed to go back to God and ask for a reduction of that number. This turned into a negotiation that went back and forth a few times and finally resulted in five prayers a day. And that is how it has remained. Now we focus on the encounter between Mohammed and Isa in the second heaven:

> Then the prophet ascended to the second heaven where Jibril again asked permission for him, and he obtained it. There he encountered Yahiah [John (the Baptist)] son of Zachariah, and Isa son of Maryam, peace be with them. He greeted them upon which they responded to him, welcomed him and acknowledged his mission. The prophet then ascended to the third heaven.

In the biography Mohammed meets Isa in the second heaven, but there are *hadith* that say that this happened in the fourth, or even fifth, heaven. There are *hadith* that describe what Jesus then looked like:

> Jesus was a ruddy man of medium height, who had lank hair and freckles on his face. His head seemed to be dripping with water, as if he had just come out of the bath.

The bath is of course the *zamzam* spring in paradise. Other *hadith* relate that pearls adorned Isa's hair.[143]

THE *IMITATIO CHRISTI*

In many *hadith* Jesus is described as the model of virtuousness and humility. He is often addressed as "Christ" or as "Spirit of God":

> Christ said: "Seeds grow in the plain, and not between rocks. Even so, wisdom flourishes in the heart of a humble man but not in the heart of a proud one. Do you not see how the man who, full of pride, wants his head to reach to the ceiling, will crush it, while he who bows his head protects it?"[144]

> If you wish, you may repeat what the Teacher of the World and of the Spirit [of God], Jesus Son of Mary, was wont to say: "Hunger is my spice, fear is my garment, wool is my dress, the light of dawn is my warmth in winter, the moon is my lantern, my legs are my beast of burden, and what the earth brings forth is my food and fruit. When night falls I withdraw without anything to my name, and in the morning I awake without anything to my name. Yet no one on earth is richer than I am."[145]

A pious Muslim will follow Jesus; at least the Sufis do that. Al-Ghazali wrote in *Ihya'ul ulum al-din* that it is better to follow Jesus than wisdom:

> Jesus said: "When one shares wisdom with those who are not worthy of it, one does wisdom an injustice; and when one withholds wisdom from those who are worthy of it, one does those an injustice. Be like a gentle physician who applies medicine to the place of illness."[146]

For Mohammed, Isa was a great example. His biography is modeled on the life of Jesus. Mohammed followed the *Imitatio Christi*.[147]

Summary

For Muslims, Isa is an important example. Isa was born from a virgin. Isa rose from the dead, ascended into heaven and may be beheld in heaven. Isa will return at the end of time. The differences with the traditional Christology of Christianity are:

1. Isa is not the Son of God (but he is called the Spirit and the Word of God);
2. In the Koran it is not clear whether Isa died and was taken up into heaven or was taken up by God; and
3. Isa certainly did not die on the cross.

Conclusion

In Christianity the death on the cross and the resurrection are conditions for the redemption of the world and the human being. This definitive redemption takes place at the end of time when Jesus Christ returns to defeat the Antichrist. As we have seen, in Islam Isa also returns to defeat the Antichrist. Therefore, whether or not he died on the cross, in both cases future redemption is in the hands of Jesus.

Part 2

The Freedom Impulse of Mohammed Abduh and Rudolf Steiner

Cilia ter Horst

Cilia ter Horst studied religion and Arabic. Her graduation thesis was on the Egyptian theologian Mohammed Abduh (1849-1905). Abduh was mufti of Egypt and a director of the Azhar, the University of Cairo. He studied theology and, during his travels through Europe, European philosophy. Abduh was an advocate of the reopening of the "gates of *ijtihad*,"* which makes the free interpretation of the Koran possible again. He focused his attention on the question of divine omnipotence versus the free will of the human being. Abduh argued that divine omnipotence and free will do not exclude each other, but presume and include each other. It is precisely the divine will and providence as laid down in the Koran, which can lead to freedom in thinking and intellectual independence of action.

As a result, Abduh may be called a philosopher of freedom. In the middle of the nineteenth century, western philosophy developed the idea that the human being is not free until he has emancipated himself from divine providence. Western philosophy is completely secularized. But this also evoked criticism, for instance, from the philosopher Rudolf Steiner (1861-1925), who founded the anthroposophical movement. In his book *The Philosophy of Freedom* the central thesis is that the human being is free only if he thinks out of the spirit.

This essay compares Abduh and Steiner: what are the similarities and differences between the philosophies of freedom of both men?

---

* Translator's note: *Ijtihad* is the making of a decision in Islamic law (*sharia*) by personal effort (*jihad*), independently of any school (*madhhab*) of jurisprudence (*fiqh*), as opposed to *taqlid*, copying or obeying without question. (Source: Wikipedia)

CHAPTER 5

Background: Types of Freedom in Mohammed Abduh's Life

Mohammed Abduh was born in 1849 in a little village in the Nile Delta in Egypt. At that time, Egypt was part of the Ottoman Empire, but it had a relatively autonomous status under the leadership of the Turkish ruler Mohammed Ali. Ali began to modernize Egypt in order to improve its deteriorating army. To pay for this he levied high taxes which made life very difficult for the peasants, to which Abduh's family belonged. The family was forced to move several times. Abduh would always remember this, and we can see it as the seed from which his aversion to oppression and foreign domination sprouted. Later he made many efforts on behalf of national independence and economic, political and social freedom.[148]

As a boy Abduh was a quick study at the Koran school in the village; when he was twelve he could recite the Koran from memory. He continued his education at the school of the mosque in Tanta, but was so unhappy with the method of instruction there, which consisted of hammering into the pupils' heads grammatical rules and Koran commentaries without any explanation, that he quit school and wanted to become a peasant like his father. An uncle of his father, Sayyid Darwish, a Sufi who had been initiated in the Shadhiliya order,[149] kept him from doing that by telling him of the mystical path.[150] He gave him texts to read and explained these for him. This awoke enthusiasm in Abduh for acquiring knowledge. He felt his earthly life becoming small and insignificant and experienced a great longing for God. Later he wrote about this uncle that he had "rescued him from the prison of ignorance into the open space of knowledge, and from the fetters of blind imitation of authoritarian faith (*taqlid*) to the freedom of the mystical union with God."[151] He went back to the school, which he now completed with more understanding than before.

At the Azhar[152] school in Cairo, where he continued his studies, he again had to cope with methods of instruction that did not offer self-developed insights, but only "slavish imitation." From the tenth century onward the conviction predominated in Islamic theology that the commentaries of the older scholars had to be adopted, and that new interpretations of the original Islamic sources were invalid, because "the gates of *ijtihad* had been closed."[153] Abduh was unable to live with this; he wanted to understand everything and did not accept knowledge without proof. Outside the theology classes he studied by himself in the library logic, philosophy and mysticism, subjects that had no priority in the curriculum of the school.

In 1871 he came into contact with Sayyid Jamal ad-Din al-Afghani during the latter's first visit to Cairo. This Iranian[154] scholar impressed Abduh because in his thinking he adopted an independent position vis-à-vis the old authorities, and he explained what he wanted to convey. Usually Abduh refused to accept anything outside mysticism, but Al-Afghani, who was himself a Sufi and more advanced on the path than Abduh, was able to convince him of the importance of western science. Abduh became Al-Afghani's best pupil and a friendship developed between them. In that period Abduh wrote about himself that "he no longer occupied himself with dogma and dialectics," and that "he was liberated from the fetters of membership in sects (the mystical order) so as to be able to strive for knowledge in freedom."[155] Thus, outside the "prison" of *taqlid*, he found intellectual freedom in the rational sciences, among which, as will be shown later, he also included true theology. After finishing his studies Abduh became a teacher, including at the Azhar school, and just like Al-Afghani, in his lessons he emphasized his own interpretations. He committed his public writing and speaking talents to working with Al-Afghani for the reformation of the Islamic world. In order to influence the opinions of Muslims they published periodicals in which they wrote articles on all kinds of social problems. They proposed a number of reforms of education, politics, social life and religion. They spread their approach to Islam as a rational religion that formed a guiding principal for all time—including modern time—provided that it would always be interpreted anew. They advocated the establishment of representative institutions, and they were fierce opponents of foreign domination.

From the sixteenth century the Ottoman Empire had deteriorated while the power of Europe had grown. One of the measures the Ottoman rulers took to strengthen their realm was to reform their armies with the help of European technology. From the end of the eighteenth century on they sent officers to Europe to be trained. They also sent intellectuals and when these came back they brought, beside technical know-how, ideas from the European enlightenment. For instance, the first Egyptian intellectual Rifa'a al-Tahtawi wrote a report of his sojourn in Paris in 1798 in which, among other things, he praised the word freedom (liberté—*hurriyya*) and gave explanations of the French parliament.

Reformist intellectuals in the Ottoman Empire debated the question of whether the conditions for a good society should be developed from European knowledge or from Islamic law. Abduh and Al-Afghani embraced modern science, but felt that European culture should not be simply copied. In their opinion, decisions as to which changes ought to be made in society and which should be avoided should be guided by criteria that could be found in the Islamic heritage. To make it possible to determine such criteria, however, Islamic theology and the actual experience of the faith needed to be reformed. In principle, the way to social security and progress was shown by the *sunna*, the tradition of the prophet handed down through the ages, but on condition that this tradition would be rightly understood. Unity among the faithful would have to be restored, and Islam would have to be understood again as the religion of rational thinking and science.

They rejected the method of *taqlid*, the adoption of old interpretations, and said that *ijtihad*, independent interpretation, should be resumed. It was their opinion that Islam was meant for all time and had to be interpreted anew all the time. The literal meaning of the word *ijtihad* is "effort"; originally it was a method to see to it that *sharia*, Islamic law, would be based as much as possible on the Koran and on *sunna*.[156] Modern thinkers, who were in touch with western thinking, developed it into a purposeful interpretation, with which Islam could be adapted to new situations.[157]

For political reasons, Abduh and Al-Afghani were exiled from Egypt, but from abroad they continued their work on their project of reforms. In Paris they founded the secret organization *al-Urwa al-Wuthqa*, "The Indissoluble Link" with which, by publishing periodicals, they attempted to influence public opinion of all Muslims in the direction of collaboration. Within a short time they became very well known, and after eighteen issues the periodical was forbidden by the French and English authorities for fear of a joint rebellion of Muslims in their colonies. Abduh taught in Beirut on the subject of *tawhid*, divine unity, which would later result in his book *Risalat al-Tawhid*, "the Message of Divine Unity."

Abduh traveled through Europe, which gave him hope and inspiration for his goal: reform in Muslim countries. Even after the end of his exile he liked to go back now and then "for renewal" and to get new ideas.[158] At an advanced age he learned French and read works by Rousseau and Renan; he admired Tolstoy to whom he wrote a letter, and Spencer whom he met. He was impressed by the many highly developed Christian charity organizations and recognized the importance of such practical public collaboration. Later, in 1892, this led him to take the lead in the foundation of the Islamic Charity Association with the goal of having Muslims work together for good causes. Many secular Islamic organizations are founded on this example, including the Muslim Brotherhood.

Abduh's relationship with Europe, however, was ambivalent because, although he did advocate development toward a better society, he wanted this to follow Islamic standards. He argued that European civilization owed its development to influences of science and philosophy from the Islamic world, and that the backwardness of the Ottoman Empire was due to the fact that the true Islam was no longer understood. His interpretation of the way in which true Islam should be understood has partly an apologetic nature, because he wanted to counter the opinions of, among others, the French historian Hanotaux and the English Lord Cromer, who said that the religion of Islam was the cause of the backwardness of the Muslim countries. He gave much attention to points on which Islam was attacked by Europeans.

After six year in exile Abduh was allowed to return to Egypt in 1888. He was treated with respect by the Egyptian people, and the authorities appointed him as *qadi*, judge at the national court of justice. He was on good terms with a part of the English government and said later that he was happy with the individual freedom that was possible as a result of the occupation.[159] In 1899 he was appointed as *mufti* of Egypt, the supreme, official interpreter of Islamic law, whose statements or *fatwas* are binding. Here also he used his reformist approach; he applied the law based on his independent judgment and made his own interpretations of the sources of Islamic law. By his free interpretation he made Islamic law applicable to all circumstances and, unlike his predecessors, he took up not only questions of government but also cases involving individuals, which often involved questions arising in modern society.

From 1895 until his death in 1905 he was a member of the leadership of the Azhar School in Cairo. In that position he succeeded in introducing a number of material changes, including fixed salaries for teachers, good facilities for the students, good classrooms and libraries, improvements in the curriculum and a reduction in the number of holidays. But in intellectual and religious respects he did not achieve all his goals. He wanted to turn Azhar into a university with all modern sciences, and wanted more leeway for individual interpretation of the Islamic sources, but he was opposed in this by the conservative leaders and Muslim scholars, who accused him of heresy because they were afraid of losing their power if his ideas were introduced. He did leave tracks with people who had followed his courses and had been inspired by him to bring new things. After his death his pupil Rashid Rida continued much of Abduh's work, although in a slightly different, more orthodox spirit.

According to Abduh and Al-Afghani the true Islam was the Islam as it was understood by the first generations of Muslims. That was the faith that had to be embraced again by the people. For this reason they founded a reform movement named Salafiya, derived from *al-salaf al-salih* (the worthy ancestors), which usually means the contemporaries and followers of the prophet. But when Abduh used the word *salaf* he referred to the central tradition of Sunni Islam in the period of its development; he included in the term *al-salaf* the great theologians of the third and fourth century of Islam, such as al-Ashari.[160] According to Hourani, one of the reasons why the Salafiya movement became more fundamentalist in nature under Rida's leadership was that Rida interpreted the term in its more usual, more limited meaning.[161]

The most important ideas that Abduh and Al-Afghani circulated in the periodical of *al-Urwa al-Wuthqa* can be summarized in five concise points:

1. Islam is corrupted by ignorance.
2. The Muslim countries have been betrayed by their leaders, because these have given too much latitude to foreigners.
3. The cure is in the return to the faith of the ancestors.
4. Islam is the religion of reason, which leads to activity and progress.
5. The people have the right of resistance against a tyrant when he ruins the country.[162]

They considered freedom and personal responsibility as important conditions for the realization of a just state under God's will. The principal quotation they invoked to justify their position was: "*Inna allaha la yughayyiru ma biqawmin hatta yughayyiru ma bi-anfusihim,*" which means: "Verily never will Allah change the condition of a people until they change it themselves (with their own souls)."[163] What is expressed here is a third form of freedom which, in Abduh's thinking, has an important role: it is the free will of the human being, freedom in a metaphysical sense. Without disavowing the omnipotence of God, Abduh and al-Afghani contended that human beings had the possibility and freedom to contribute to their own happiness. In this they ran counter to the prevailing belief in the unfreedom of the human being.

Unlike his teacher, Abduh did not interpret the above quotation from the Koran as a call to political revolution. The verse indicates that the people must themselves begin with making changes but that, in the end, God determines their condition. Abduh recognized that it was not within his power or time to transform Egypt into an independent—let alone, democratic—state. He considered a political struggle for this goal as a building without foundation as long as the people were not adequately educated.[164] For a long time he pondered the difference between the right of the government to obedience of the people and the right of the people to a just government. He called on the people to be conscious of their rights vis-à-vis the government: a human ruler can make mistakes and has to be corrected by guidelines given to him by the people. But later, says Rida in his biography of Abduh, he left the question of political authority in the hands of destiny and of God, "because he realized that in such matters, nations harvest the fruits of trees they have planted themselves and have nurtured for years and years, while he now had to concern himself with planting seeds, with God's help."[165] For him this meant that he had to dedicate himself to the education of the people.

In his own words, Abduh devoted himself during his life to two great objectives. The first was the liberation of the spirit from the fetters of slavish imitation, *taqlid*, so that the faith would again be understood in the same way as by the first followers of the prophet before any schisms had grown, as a God-given completion of reason.[166] The second great objective was reform of the Arabic language. The language had become too complicated and he wanted to reform it in such a way that everyone could read the newspaper.

The point of departure in Abduh's thinking lay in the decadence of the Muslim world and therefore its need of restoration. Both in political and in moral respects, the Ottoman empire showed signs of decadence while, on the other hand, the European countries were becoming more and more powerful. As a faithful Muslim, Abduh dreamed of the day when the world of Islam would once again be a strong counterweight over against the power of Europe. He believed that this could happen if Muslims would find their true faith again and the community of the faithful (*umma*) became one again. At the same time, he was a nationalist who dreamed of an Egyptian state liberated from the Turkish dominance that he remembered from his youth as the oppressor of his parents. Thus while, on the one hand, he preached the importance of unity among all Muslims, on the other hand, he adhered to the European idea of the nation state for every nation with a common language and history. The paradox appears stronger than it is. Abduh said that there had to be unanimity among the faithful as to the established elements of the faith, and Muslims and Muslim nations had to support each other, but they did not need to exist under one secular leader. The leader of the *umma*, as he imagined it, was a *mujtahid*, an interpreter. For the secular order, nationalism was inevitable as the element that binds the people together and, in the final analysis, the best form of government was one in which the people were represented through a parliament.[167]

Within the nation state it was even more important that there be unity. In Egypt, Abduh saw a dangerous gap growing between the traditional Islamic spirit that was opposed to any change, and the younger generation that applauded all change and embraced the ideals of the French Revolution. In order to close this gap, he showed that modernization was in accord with Islam, and that Islam was a good guide in the life of the human being in modern society. It was his opinion that modernization of society was necessary in order to compete with the Europeans, but that it had to take place in harmony with Islam. Egypt could not simply adopt European culture; the difference between the two cultures was too great. Such a sudden turn would be unnatural and therefore dangerous. That was manifest in the Egyptian elite, which wished to adopt free thinking and the concept of freedom from Europe, but was driven by desire and lust because Egyptian society was not ready to comprehend the meaning of freedom.[168]

Muslims had to change their mental attitude, throw superstition overboard and learn western technology to defend themselves, but this development had to take place gradually and out of their own culture. Abduh viewed Islam as the absolute standard by which to judge the question of whether a change should or should not be adopted. He said that everything was subject to natural laws, and that violating those laws would lead to deterioration and decadence. In human society these were the moral laws that framed human behavior and had to have a relationship with society. If a people would imitate another people with which it did not really have a close relationship, it would lose its own essential character. In due course this would lead to the demise of that country. For Egypt this meant that Islam could not be denied. The Egyptian "folk soul" was so deeply permeated by religion that "the education of the Egyptian people without religion would be like planting a seed in the wrong kind of soil, so that it would be unable to sprout."[169]

Abduh saw no reason to turn away from Islam on the way to a just and good form of government. The ethics of Islam were exactly was what needed for the education of the individual, family and nation. It taught people that they had freedom and how they should use this freedom in the right way. Long ago, the Arabians had established a flourishing culture and a powerful empire by building on the foundations laid by the prophets. The same was true for all nations that had achieved such power and culture: they had achieved it purely by following their religious laws, for the laws that served the common good were those of religious education.

Abduh viewed religion as the element that binds people together in society, and he believed that Islam was pre-eminently in harmony with the intellect and progress, because it strove to liberate the spirit from superstition, and gave humanity a divine law that was also the law of nature.[170] His ideas have been compared with those of Comtean positivism.[171] Auguste Comte (1798-1857) searched for a rational morality that would be able to take over the connecting function of religion in modern times, and Abduh did everything he could to show that Islam had in it the potential of the rational religion that was needed, namely morality and social science. Influenced as he was by theories of natural law and utilitarianism, he viewed Islam as the true sociology, the moral law that guided humanity in such a way that it would bring prosperity to human society:

> Religion is the first teacher and the best leader for souls to acquire the sciences and broaden knowledge. It is the most gentle educator and the most far-seeing thinker, which lifts souls to the highest virtues and the best characters.[172]

According to Abduh the people should receive religious education by social class. For the lowest class a stable faith that led to activity was sufficient; the intelligentsia had to be able to interpret the Koran and the *sunna* independently with the help of modern science. This meant that the religion had to be reformed, because the way in which Islam was experienced and practiced in his time went counter to activity and science. It was the essence of Islam as it was originally intended which embodied these principles and stimulated them in the faithful, Abduh believed. How this works is described in his book *Risalat al-Tawhid*.

CHAPTER 6

Between God and Nature: Human Free Will According to Rudolf Steiner and Mohammed Abduh

Introduction

During the time that Rudolf Steiner wrote *The Philosophy of Freedom* in Germany (1893), Mohammed Abduh was lecturing in Lebanon about divine unity (1883). These lectures were collected in his book *Risalat al-Tawhid* (1897), Message of Unity. Both thinkers, each in their own way, contended that the human being has free will. Steiner reacted against the thought that the human being is fully determined by physical laws; Abduh against the idea that the human being is completely directed by God. What is the nature of human free will according to each of them, and what is its basis?

Rudolf Steiner: The Basis of Thinking

The Austrian Rudolf Steiner was a thirty-year-old philosopher in Germany when he wrote a book about the core questions of philosophy; he gave it the title *The Philosophy of Freedom*.[173] He wrote it (in part) in reaction to his contemporary, the philosopher Eduard von Hartmann, who argued that human freedom is an illusion. People imagine themselves free, said Hartmann, because they are not aware of the blind will which works in creation, society and the human being. The "absolute unconscious" is the grounds of existence.[174]

Countering this, Steiner contended that one can also perform actions which are not caused out of the unconscious, but are inspired by a conscious motive.

According to him, we can learn through universal thinking, which precedes the split between subject and object, to receive insights or intuitions from the spiritual world and to act on these in the physical world. When we succeed in this we act, according to Steiner, on our own accord, out of free will.

Steiner begins his book in a natural scientific and philosophic context with the question: "Is the human being spiritually *free*, or subject to the iron necessity of natural law?"[175] This evokes a number of questions: Is the human being a spiritual being? And is he free in this spiritual aspect? Or does "spiritual" by definition mean free? What is the influence of natural law? Is it possible to be determined spiritually by natural law?

It is not immediately clear whether he places "spiritual" in opposition to "determined by natural law," or "free" in opposition to "determined." Later in the book, however, it becomes evident that for Steiner spiritual and free belong together, because he views the human being as a spiritual being to the extent that the latter is, as an individual, connected with "the spiritual world," a genuinely existing world of concepts to which the human being has access through his intuition.

For Steiner, freedom is in a certain sense an intervention in matter by the spirit through an act of an individual human being. This does not involve complying with a generally accepted norm, but a self-generated "invention" of such a norm through the medium of moral imagination, i.e., through receiving intuitions from the spirit.

The question as to human freedom can be reformulated as: Can the human being influence his thinking and acting out of the spirit, out of a desire that is not determined by natural law? And if so, is he spiritually independent or is there something else that brings him into movement?

Steiner's answer is that thinking is independent. It is through thinking that we ask, and answer, all these questions; therefore it is thinking on which all knowledge depends. It can generate itself and understand itself. Moreover, conscious thinking, in the sense of actively making thoughts our own, is an activity of the "I." It contains activity of will. And the other way around, nothing is willed which is not experienced by this "I," while it is thinking, as its own clearly structured activity.[176] The will is therefore defined as "originating in thinking, which is independent and is an activity of the 'I,'" so that the "I" determines the will and the thinking, and in that sense the "I" is autonomous and possesses a free will that is entirely at its disposal.

However, the will as it is meant here must be distinguished from the kind of will that, in our daily use of the word, is often attributed to a human being who acts out of necessity or passion. And the thinking described here must be distinguished from the usual automatic kind of thinking, which really consists of the observation of thought images that arise in the soul all by themselves.[177] In brief, the will and thinking are matters of the intellect, which is individual, independent, autonomous: free.

In his preface to the 1918 edition of *The Philosophy of Freedom* Steiner emphasizes his intention once more with the pointed questions:

First, can we understand human nature in such a way that this understanding serves as the basis for everything else we may meet in the way of experience or science?

And

Second, can we human beings, as willing entities, ascribe freedom to ourselves, or is this freedom a mere illusion that arises because we do not see the threads of necessity upon which our willing, like any other natural event, depends?[178]

Then he explains that he attempts to demonstrate that it is possible to penetrate into human nature so deeply that all one's other knowing can be grounded in this insight, and that this insight justifies the idea of a free will, "provided that one finds the region of the soul where free will can develop."[179] Next, he tries to justify rationally that we can have knowledge of the realm of spirit by demonstrating that unbiased investigation, which is focused on the above two questions, leads to the conviction that the human being lives in a genuinely spiritual world.[180]

In summary: by finding a) a fixed point, and b) the region in the soul where the free will can unfold, it is possible to justify 1) the reality of the spiritual world, and 2) the free will.

Something therefore precedes the possibility of freedom. Free will does not simply exist, it has to arise—in a "region of the soul." With talent and exercise, the human being is able to learn to receive thoughts that have not been formed by physical impulses. Steiner calls the organ through which thoughts can thus be received "intuition," the contents of which consist of free thoughts that were not determined by natural laws, but were created out of the spirit.

Steiner calls these contents "moral imagination." Regarding morality, which is the second theme of *The Philosophy of Freedom*, he speaks of "ethical individualism." True morality, he says, is *spiritual desire*. It is not imposed, but intrinsically present in the human being. In order to be moral, human beings must not follow a moral order that exists independently of themselves—morally acting human beings strive after their own motives, which they themselves have generated in freedom. These are ideas out of a *spiritual* world, which is not an illusory thought, but an actual world that is observable with non-physical senses. It is a world in which all human beings take part, and which is one, so that the ideas proceeding from it foster unity, and are therefore not destructive but always constructive—and in that sense moral—even if we often cannot recognize that right away. For instance, such ideas may go against prevailing norms and destroy something temporary, but have a healthy effect later. Every individual has different intuitions, but these never work against each other. When people live out of pure intuition, they follow their own will and yet they never get into conflict.

Steiner sounds warnings against relinquishing our own free will. That does not lead to morality but to imitation. This may be all right for the "lower passions," for physical desires, but not for spiritual longing, desire prompted by intuitive thinking that is free from the restraints of the physical. Spiritual desire has to be followed; it is constructive for the world and humanity.

Degrees of Moral Action

Human deeds are caused by something. Every human deed has a driving force, a cause. Steiner explores these causes and divides them into four categories, from unfree to free.

At the most basic level, an action is initiated very directly by passion. Such an action immediately follows on a certain perception, for instance the perception of hunger and the instinct of survival. The perception and the passion form the *motive* for the action, for instance eating.

At the second level, feelings and emotions are the motive; a feeling of compassion can thus be the motive for offering consolation to someone.

At the third level, thinking and imagination enter into the picture. Steiner calls this practical experience. For instance, the imagination of a particular enjoyment may motivate a person to make an effort to achieve it.

The fourth level of motivation is that of thinking in concepts independent of the content of perception. This occurs through pure thinking or practical reason, and it involves concepts that have been learned, for instance, in shared norms and values.

The characteristic of human beings who are becoming free is that they can learn to recognize *why* they allow themselves to be governed by a particular rule. This can lead to making a step from morality based on authority to acting out of ethical insight. This again involves mental pictures or concepts, including mental pictures of feelings (for instance, the imagination of wellbeing), but now in the form of personal ideals, which Steiner calls *motives* of moral action. These can be distinguished as follows:

Fostering the wellbeing of humanity.
Fostering the moral and cultural development of humanity.
Intuitively discovered moral goals, ideal intuitions.

The step from morality based on authority to acting out of ethical insight is, according to Steiner, a step forward in the moral development of the human being. Human beings can in due course become free and, out of insight, do the good in freedom. Before they reach that stage, however, they need norms and values to give direction to their deeds and to prevent society, and themselves, from falling apart. As long as human beings are not free they have to be *compelled* to their actions.[181] Whether this takes place through outer coercion or moral direction makes no difference in principle. Human beings are free only when they follow their own intuition.

In the fourth driving force and the third motive, driving force and motive coincide: longing and ideal overlap. At this level, an action results neither from a rulebook nor from an external occasion in some automatic fashion. It is determined exclusively by the idea content, not by the external environment, but inspired out of the individual spirit, and therefore free.[182] An intuition arises in a person which becomes the driving force of a deed. Neither directly (from some event) nor indirectly (from morality that was learned from others) is such a deed determined by external circumstances. The acting person decides in his or her heart how to act. This is what Steiner calls the *truly individual will*.

Individual and Thinking

Thus we see that an inspiration that truly originates with the spirit is free from physical laws. But how exactly does this come about? What does "originating with the spirit" mean? Does that mean "from the individual"? Or could it, for instance, have been prompted by a spiritual being outside the individual? And in this case, can it still be called "free," i.e., free from "spiritual laws"? Or do we have to conclude that for Steiner "free" only means that spiritual ideas can work on earth through an individual? And that those ideas were perhaps not developed by that individual, but were certainly thought by him or her?

The individual is then, one could say, a door between one world and another, and freedom lies in the ability to be open or closed to this possibility.

There is still another way in which freedom continues to exist. We have seen how, according to Steiner, we can learn to notice how a thought arises in us. Since we have already shown that a deed of which we do not know the driving force cannot be free, we need to discuss only thoughts that are in our consciousness. As soon as something is in our consciousness we know what it is and where it comes from: did we create it ourselves, or was it suddenly there? If we get an inspiration we are able to notice this and identify it as a thought that did not originate with ourselves. On the other hand, what Steiner calls *free thinking* is "live": it takes place at the moment when it is perceived—the thoughts are formed and received at the same time. Free thinking is self-creating, it proceeds from itself. The *freely thinking* individual *creates* thoughts.

Individuals who can think in this way arrive at a way of thinking in the spirit that is one: everything that is thought in them is also thought by them. At that level, everyone's consciousness is one, all consciousness is one, there is only one consciousness, so that such individuals can justifiably say "I think" while it can at the same time be said that "it thinks in them."

Talent, environment and exercises will contribute to the extent to which individuals are capable of bringing self-created motives to realization; the motives themselves are not determined by anyone or anything outside themselves, rather they have their origin in the individuals themselves. If these self-created thoughts now become motives or driving forces, and the individuals succeed in acting in accordance with them, they act out of self-created causes and not, therefore, out of anything external: *free.*

And yet, we are still left with questions. Are not spiritual individuals formed by certain forces just like their physical bodies? How did they come into being and how did they develop? Why does one individual create one motive and another individual a different one? Did they arise out of themselves? Who are these spiritual individuals? We get no answers to these questions.

THE FREEDOM IMPULSE OF MOHAMMED ABDUH AND RUDOLF STEINER

Summary

We have seen that thinking stands on its own. When we observe our thinking and wonder who it is who thinks, we discover that it is we ourselves who think. In such self-exploration it becomes evident that most thoughts are reactions to perceptions made in the world around us. But the choice we have when we become conscious of this is free relative to our surroundings. In such cases, the choice against or in favor of a particular action depends on individual will. There is no other reason for the action than "because I do it." It is a creative choice, an exploration, a leap into the dark; it is playing: doing something and viewing afterward what effect it has. That is also how it is with thinking. For some thoughts the question of why we are thinking them cannot be answered. The surest statement we can make of such a thought is: "I think it." We are then thinking thoughts in the playful, self-creating manner mentioned above.

We have also seen that human individuals can develop themselves in such a way that they become able to perform deeds that are not determined by external physical causes. To achieve this, they must have found the right region in the soul where free will is able to unfold.

We have not seen how thinking and the individual came into being, and can therefore not say whether there are perhaps (spiritual) reasons that have conditioned us and determine how we play.

ABDUH: DIVINE UNITY AND HUMAN CAPACITIES

The Islamic theologian Mohammed Abduh (1849-1905) lectured to theology students in Lebanon during the period in which he was exiled from his home country of Egypt. His subject was the *tawhid*, the belief in the unity of God. It was in the time when the power of the Ottoman empire was waning while that of Christian Europe was growing, and Arabic intellectuals were discussing why that was happening. Some of them thought that the Muslim faith was the cause of the Ottoman decline, while others argued that, on the contrary, it was caused by the lack of a correct faith in Islam. Abduh belonged to the second group, although he embraced western philosophy and integrated this in his interpretation of the correct faith of Islam.

For Abduh, in his orthodox Muslim context, the question of free human will was not a search for a will free of natural laws, as it was for Steiner, but a will that was able to operate autonomously, separately from God. Many people around him believed that every human deed was directed by God, a higher power who had everything in his hand, and that it would be proof of unbelief to think that the human being took an active part in events.

M. W. Watt[183] sees in this a remnant of the pre-Islamic fatalism of Arabian culture, where the conviction reigned that everything that happened had been written down beforehand in a heavenly book. The device was: "Eat, drink and be happy, for tomorrow you may be dead."[184] The message of the Koran counters this by stating that after death all human beings are individually rewarded or punished for their deeds by a personal God, and are thus able to contribute to their own happiness by doing good. But fatalistic thinking continued to exist, and was in the course of the history of Muslim theology taken up in Muslim doctrine, such as the Christian doctrine of predestination.[185] In contradistinction to this, Abduh contended that human beings had been created with intellect and will and that good faith presumed that one made use of one's God-given capacities and actively carried one's own responsibility.

Abduh's book *Risalat al Tawhid* begins with a description of God and His attributes, which include:

1. Perfect knowledge (*ilm*), for nothing escapes Him.
2. Will (*irada*), for He has given everything its specific properties and purpose in accord with His knowledge.
3. Omnipotence (*qudra*), the capacity of action, the power to execute His will.
4. Freedom of choice (*ikhtiyar*), for everything proceeds from Him in accordance with His knowledge, will and actions (knowledge, will and power imply freedom, which is: independently creating some thing in accordance with knowledge and will).[186]
5. Unity (*wahda*); nothing is His equal, for if there were other powers their wills would come into conflict with each other and the order of the universe would fall apart, and that is not the case.

God's omnipotence means that everything that is, is as it is because it is His will. Since He has perfect knowledge, He knows everything in advance. He takes all consequences of His deeds into account in the decisions of His will. Therefore, His will is not fickle, it does not change from moment to moment. As a result, the causes and effects we observe in nature remain the same, even though they are subject to His will.[187] He has created nature and its fixed laws, and He has given all creatures their specific properties. His promises and retributions are executed of necessity because they are part of His perfect knowledge, will and truth.

Abduh then investigates the powers of the human being, including the will, feeling and thinking. By nature, human beings strive for perfection, harmony and happiness. They know of themselves that they exist and are able to make rational choices.[188] They consider their deeds with their intellect (*aql*), decide them with their will (*irada*) and bring them to realization with a force they possess for that purpose (*qudra*). But they do not always succeed in achieving things in accordance with their will. The consequences of their deeds do not always pan out the way these were intended. This may be caused by human beings' own fault or incapacity, by opposition from a rival, by events of nature or other, inexplicable reasons. Such factors lead them to the idea that there exists a power outside of themselves, over which they have no control.[189] The facts will give them the insight that all occurrences in the world proceed totally from a necessary Being (the first cause of everything) which has determined all events out of His will and knowledge. Human beings will then recognize their own position and subject themselves to the higher power with humility and reverence. But at the same time, they will not forget that they themselves also play a role in the occurrence of events, because of the powers they have received from God and for which they should be thankful to Him.[190]

Abduh simply posits that human beings have the power to choose their deeds in accordance with their knowledge and will but that, at the same time, God is omnipotent. He gets himself out of this theological dilemma by pointing out that the precise relationship between divine power and human choice is contained in the secret of predestination (*sirr al-qadar*), which is hidden from our intellect and with which we must not concern ourselves.[191] Those Christians and Muslims who did occupy themselves with it had endless discussions about it, but they eventually circled back to the place where they started and did nothing but sow discord.

> Let me say again, faith in the Divine unity requires from the believer only that his powers are from God's hand, that he "acquires" his faith and the other religious works which God has enjoined, that the power of God transcends all human competence and has alone the supreme authority over all the desires of men and their realization, whether by voiding the obstacles or ordering the operative factors which elude the knowledge or the will of man. To pursue the matter further and pry into its mysterious elements is, as we have shown, no part of the province of faith.[192]

There have been occasional individuals who understood it better, but God gives the light of understanding only according to His will. For the masses such speculation is dangerous and confusing and it is harmful for the current condition of society.

Abduh strengthens the idea that he adopts a middle position between predestination and human free will by using the term *kasb*,* "acquisition," the concept with which theologians attempted to reconcile the points of view of the Jabarites (predestination) and Qadarites (free will): God creates the deed and He enables the human being to bring it to realization. It is dangerous for Abduh to state this in a Sunni environment; it will expose him to accusations of the sin of *shirk*, which consists either of making the human being a partner of God or placing something on a level with God. Abduh interprets this sin in a different way. He says that it means, for instance, attributing certain forces to stars and stones in lieu of relying only on one's God-given capacities and asking God for help when these are insufficient.

> All creatures have their peculiar characteristics. Human beings are amidst these. Among the distinguishing features by which they are different from other animals are their capacity for thought and their ability to choose actions in line with their thinking. It is with their being, as given to them, that these distinctive qualities belong. If they were to be deprived of any of them they would become, perhaps, angels, or some animal. When we say that people are human with that gift of being which is humanity, this in no way means that there is any compulsoriness about their actions. The Divine knowledge is the context of what the human will effectuates. It is aware they will do such and such action at such and such a time—a good deed to be rewarded, for example, and that they will do this or that evil and be appropriately requited. Their works are throughout the consequence of their "acquisitions" and choices. Nothing in (Divine) knowledge dispossesses human beings of their option-taking in "acquisitions."[193] The fact that what is in the Divine knowledge must inevitably befall arises from its being actual, and that which is so is not susceptible of being changed.[194]

Divine omniscience is so real that it is impossible that it would not come true. God therefore knows in advance what human beings will do with their free will; nevertheless human beings really have this free will.[195]

---

* Translator's note: A doctrine in Islam adopted by the theologian Al-Ashari (d. 935) as a mean between predestination and free will. According to Al-Ashari all actions, good and evil, are originated by God, but they are "acquired" by human beings. (Source: Wikipedia)

Again, as to the will of the human being, there is no doubt that we possess it, says Abduh:

> The man of sound mind and sense knows and affirms of himself that he exists and needs no guide or teacher to bring him to this conclusion. It is the same precisely with his awareness of his actions of will. He weighs them and their consequences in his mind and evaluates them in his will, and then effectuates them by an inner power. To deny any of this would be tantamount to a denial of his existence itself, so opposed would it be to rational evidence. [196]

But human beings observe that they cannot obtain everything they want, and thus develop the idea of a higher power that has everything in his hand. They continue to recognize their own contribution to the course of events, but in reality the capacities with which they choose their deeds originate with God. This means that God is indeed omnipotent, but the human being has the faculty of action, freedom and responsibility.

As to self-knowledge, according to Abduh human beings know for certain that they are living beings with feeling and will. Other observations are derived from this. However, the essence of the human being is inaccessible to knowledge. Language does not "grasp" the truth and does not do justice to how things are in their essence. Thinking can know the causes and classifications and principles of things, but has no rational access to the essence of things. Nor do human beings need this, for it suffices that they know the events and qualities. Searching for the essence is a waste of time.

Good and Evil Deeds

About the origin of the concepts of good and evil Abduh says the following: they are connected with an intuitive preference for the perfect, the beautiful, the life-giving, and an aversion to imperfection and decadence. Human beings, therefore, find in themselves the ability to distinguish between beautiful and ugly. People may have different opinions about some things, however: "Tastes may differ, but things are either beautiful or ugly."[197]

The voluntary deeds of human beings belong to the category of what exists in actual fact, and human beings experience them, just like physical things, as beautiful or ugly. This is the basis of the distinction between sin and virtue. A good deed is a contribution to perfection, i.e., beauty and wellbeing;[198] an evil deed does harm to this and causes chaos. There are good (or beautiful or pleasant) deeds that have bad consequences, and there are evil (or ugly or annoying) deeds that have good consequences. In order to explore what deeds are to their advantage, human beings have received the capacities of memory, imagination and reflective thinking. These properties distinguish them from animals. They are the basis of man's happiness but, at the same time, they are the source of his distress.[199] They vary from one human being to another—one has higher capacities than another.

Leadership

With their memory, imagination and reflective thinking, human beings can thus decide whether any deed is good or evil both in itself and as to its consequences. Human happiness depends on these capacities. The quality of these capacities differs from one person to another and is in part determined by someone's temperament and personal surroundings. But for exceptional cases, people are generally not able to obtain happiness completely through their intellect. One way or another, they end up in situations where they tend toward evil, even though they strive for the good. This is true for life on earth, and even more so for the hereafter, when we do not know the consequences of the deeds we commit today, while everyone does know through intuition that the soul continues to exist after life on earth.[200] Only in very rare cases have human beings received such a perfect intellect and "light of perception" that, without the guidance and example of a prophet, they are able to have knowledge of God and can lead humanity. These are the prophets.

A prophetic mission is possible, for people differ in intelligence, and therefore, why should not some people be all-knowing? What reason is for the individual, a prophet is for humanity. Exceptional individuals are knowing and participate in the prophetic message. The masses do not. People would be capable of living together if they were able to live out of pure love. Because they are not able to do this, and also do not have an instinct in other ways for what the community needs, but all have their own thoughts and desires, they are in need of leadership from a revelation that convinces both intelligent and ignorant or proud people and prompts them to good deeds.

For this reason, God has created a number of human beings with such a perfect intelligence that they have access to both realities: prophets. Prophets share in the glory of God but are, at the same time, fully human and exposed to ordinary human experiences. They lead the human spirit to knowledge of God and the necessary knowledge of His attributes. They teach people how they should honor

God. They proclaim that human society is based on love through which one respects the rights of everyone and helps one another.

Degrees of Moral Action

People differ in their abilities to understand and in their capacities to act. The first group Abduh recognizes is that of "the ones who fall short."[201] They are lazy or weak, but have many desires. They find pleasure in enjoyments without working. The impulse of a thought or picture of pain or joy prompts them to action. Fraud and violence determine their deeds, and they are governed by the pursuit of bodily delights.

The second group has spiritual ambitions. They enjoy being praised, a need that may be very strong. This is a positive factor for the acquisition of virtues and for stabilizing relationships among people, provided it is used in the right way. But it can also turn to perversity and abuse. Intimidation and fear mongering are then the results.

With these two groups a community cannot exist; it would disintegrate. The human species needs love, or an active equivalent, for its continuing existence. Some people have found this in righteousness. Reason would be able to decide what this is. Just as thinking, memory and imagination may be sources of misery, they may also bring happiness and rest. One can train oneself to evaluate everything, to distinguish temporary discomfort from lasting happiness, to investigate the consequences of deeds and develop perseverance so as not immediately to follow one's passions, but to strive for lasting happiness. These are the principles of virtue and vice.

Thinkers have formulated these principles and authorities have tried to inculcate them into the masses. But this is unachievable, because the majority of people do not recognize what is good, they are unable to distinguish worthiness from ignorance, and are not inclined to follow someone merely because one speaks the truth. Rational proof does not prevent conflict. Moreover, the instinctive sense, which lives in everyone, that there exists a power greater than we, has a much deeper quality and stronger power of conviction. Everyone searches for this power; everyone wants to know what it is. People have looked for it in the animal world, in the stars, in trees and rocks and in certain forces. But more subtle thinking and a more penetrating consciousness has made the ideas transcendent, with more finely distinguished consequences, and finally one arrived at the idea of that which necessarily *is*. Nevertheless, aspects of omnipotence continued to remain veiled, and no one has had the power to lead humanity, so that conflicting theories have continued to exist and true leadership is rarely followed. There was agreement on the idea that one had to subject oneself to the higher power, but not on how exactly this would have to be done.

Human beings need community, but have no instinct for what a community needs. They are trapped in a web of their own ideas. They ascend with their thinking to high divine power, but drop down into deep depths when they cannot penetrate something. Only the enlightened (*al-mustabsirun*) have the key. It is precisely their weakness which has led human beings to truth. Out of humility they rise to honor and wellbeing. God has given humanity a gift which takes on the role of love: revelation through guides and mentors who are convincing for everyone; they sharpen the intellect of the intelligentsia and overpower the ignorant. They knock at the doors of our hearts. To subject ourselves to them is a necessity more than a carefully considered decision of our will. They teach people what God has entrusted to them for their wellbeing.

In brief, according to Abduh, the relevance of religion lies in the fact that average people cannot be brought to acting morally through logic. Some people are able to keep up with the laws of happiness with their intellect, but these are exceptional cases. The intellectuals cannot convince the masses, who are at a different level of intelligence, of their ideas of norms and values.[202] Religion is the strongest factor for public and private ethics. Faith in God and His laws reaches all of humanity; it exercises authority in the human soul greater than reason, despite the human being's unique rational capacities.[203] This does not mean that religion does reason an injustice, or that religion is based on pure subjection and is inimical to rational research. If that were so, religion could not be a means to guide the human being.[204] But once one has acknowledged the mission of a prophet, one is obliged to accept everything the prophet brings, even if one cannot understand everything. However, this obligation does not include having to accept rational impossibilities, for prophets do not proclaim such. If there seems to be a contradiction in the revelation, its apparent meaning is not the same as its intended one. In such cases, reason can choose to search for the true intention by referring to the rest of the revelation, or by falling back on God and His omniscience.[205]

Evolution

Individuals and communities are always in a continual process of development that is directed by divine wisdom. This is the cause of the differences in divine worship and the patterns of religion that have arisen through the ages. For God gives humanity all that is needed for this, which is why every people and every epoch has a fitting faith. In this way He provides for humanity on its path from ignorance to mature intelligence. The first religion, Judaism, was simple; it was based on obedience and not on understanding. The second religion, Christianity, given later when humanity had acquired more self-consciousness, was more sensitive and taught selflessness and an orientation toward higher spheres. Then came Islam, which turned to reason and preferred the inner over the outer aspects of faith. Islam teaches the unity of God. This doctrine of divine unity shows the human being how to serve only God's purpose and no longer to be bound to others. He obtained the right of being a free human being among free human beings, with personal responsibility and without differences in status. All that counted was good deeds and intelligence.

> The only drawing near to God was by the path of utter purity of mind, with sincerity and integrity of deed.[206]

And Sura 53:39:

> ... Human beings shall have nothing but what they strive for.

Islam only prohibits things that are bad for the individual or the community; within these limits, it leaves human beings free in fulfilling their needs. The human being has therefore received independence of will, thinking and opinion.

> Hereby, and from all the foregoing, human beings entered into two great possessions relating to religion, which had for too long been denied them, namely independence of will and independence of thought and opinion.[207] By these human beings were perfected. By these they were put in the way of attaining that happiness which God had prepared for them in the gift of mind.[208]

Human beings must use their minds and carefully consider everything they hear before either accepting or rejecting it, no matter who the speaker is. *Taqlid*, slavish imitation, is therefore forbidden.

Islam is the ultimate, mature form of religion. In Islam, all human beings are equal and each one learns what is best for him or her; the way to God is clear, and the meaning of the rites is rationally understandable. The rules bring freedom of thinking, intellectual independence of action, and therefore integrity of character, enhancement of capacities and a general revival of intention and success.[209] When the wisdom of the Koran is properly valued, discord will disappear; people will collaborate in fellowship and guard the truth.

The key elements are the unity of God and rational thinking of the human being: every human being creates his and her own activity, but only God has the highest authority. Because of Islam human beings have become free and respectable: the will was freed from the bonds that kept them bound to the will of others, whether other human beings, gods or things like stones and stars—human spirits were liberated out of the slavery imposed by frauds and swindlers. From now on human beings serve only God. The faithful must honor and obey God and try to understand His message. The Koran leaves the precise application to intelligent human beings.

In brief: according to Abduh, human beings are not all-powerful and therefore not completely free. There are things which they cannot obtain. They should seek help in the one and only highest authority, divine unity. Human beings are independent of their fellow humans and of the power of stones and stars, but they are dependent on God. Human beings have their own innate capacities, including a certain measure of free will, which can grow to the extent that they purify their thoughts and deeds; these capacities are, however, bestowed on them by the divine unity.

Conclusion

For Steiner the highest achievable freedom is: to bring ideal intuitions to realization. For Abduh it is: to follow intuitively sensed and rationally understood insights, with the help of prophets. For both, the extent of freedom depends on capacities that differ for each individual.

Abduh calls on a group of theology students to interpret the Koran themselves and to make themselves independent of their fellow human beings and of their passions. This is a step toward more freedom than slavishly adopting the interpretations of others. Steiner writes for scientifically thinking readers: you have to find a region in your soul where your free will is able to unfold, and learn to become conscious of your intuitions and bring them to realization.

Abduh says that, as a rule, one should allow oneself to be persuaded by convincing reasoning, but that there are some things which one is not able to evaluate, so that one simply has to accept these. Abduh encourages people not just to believe but also to understand and not just accept the things they are told. He was himself someone who did not want to accept but wanted to understand. Even as a child he had great difficulties accepting methods of instruction in which understanding was not fostered. But he does not completely reject

THE FREEDOM IMPULSE OF MOHAMMED ABDUH AND RUDOLF STEINER

faith which he views as the best educator of humanity; moreover, he considers it irrational to reject it completely because his intuition tells him that behind all phenomena hides a unity beyond comprehension.[210]

Steiner says that in our time people want to understand things for themselves, so that they *know* instead of *believe*. He does try to connect a deeper experience to intellectual knowledge. He does not throw scientific methods and social and religious rules overboard, because as long as the right region in the human soul has not awakened, where free, intrinsically moral will comes into being; people need rules so they will do the good.

Steiner evokes the question in us whether learning to follow intuitions does not resemble following "His will," as it is often expressed in Christian tradition. As one climbs the steps of moral action from impulsive self-satisfaction to conscious intuitive action, is not "my will" step-by-step transformed into "*the* will," namely the will of spiritual unity? And if so, does this mean a diminution of individuality and, therefore, of personal freedom? Or does the liberated human being, who is now a true individual, always remain conscious of self, albeit following "the will," but consciously and continually choosing to do so?

We also find the change from "my will" to "His will" or "the will" in Sufism into which Abduh was initiated in his youth by his uncle, and with which he became more familiar later through his Persian teacher al-Afghani.[211] According to today's Iranian philosopher Shabestari, this movement of a growing experience of unity need not imply the surrender of the human being. Shabestari says: becoming one with God is an affirmation of the human being.[212]

Both thinkers speak positively about human free will and view it as a possibility of doing the good. Ethical deeds proceed from intuition and can only take place in freedom. Both thinkers also contend that the human being must progress through a number of stages on his way to a condition in which he can exercise his free will. From the moment when he relinquishes direct self-satisfaction on this path he is in need of support, which can come from outer laws or from internalized acquired ideas about good and evil. Such ideas may arise out of practice or out of tradition handed on by people (Steiner), or they may have been revealed by certain persons with a very special intelligence—prophets (Abduh). The achievement of freedom consists of the ability to think and decide for the good out of oneself. Absolute freedom is: doing something without there being an external cause or need (Steiner), or: generating something out of oneself in accordance with knowledge and will (Abduh). Steiner looks for these external causes in natural laws, Abduh in super-earthly forces and God. Steiner speaks of a spirit which is one and to which human beings can obtain access by developing special capacities; Abduh speaks of an eternal being which is one and which speaks to human beings through special capacities that are more developed in some persons than in others, most of all in prophets. Both thinkers conclude that human beings are able to develop a certain measure of freedom and autonomy, but can never become all-powerful. Human beings may be able to make decisions out of themselves, but they lack the forces to actually bring everything to realization.

Part 3

The Philosophy of Freedom in Iranian Islam

Christine Gruwez

Christine Gruwez is a philosopher and studied Iranian languages and culture. In the following essay she discusses a number of Iranian philosophers who, through the centuries, have been in search of freedom. Philosophy is popular in Iran. Iranian philosophy is not the same thing as Islamic philosophy. In the background behind Iranian philosophy stands always the old Persian culture, as well as ancient philosophy such as Neoplatonism. Iranian philosophy, and Islamic philosophy in general, are very different from western philosophy. There are at least two fundamental differences which will be highlighted in this essay.

First, in Iranian philosophy the separation between subject and object is maintained much less strictly as the basis of cognition than is the case in western philosophy. In fact, according to the modern Iranian philosopher Yazdi (1923-1999) the famous words of Descartes "I think" (therefore I am) do not mean that the "I" thinks, but that "it" thinks. For "it," as subject, can be placed over against "thinking" as object, but "I" cannot. The "I" does not stand over against thinking, but *is the thinking itself.* The "I" is the thinking, and therefore does not stand over against thinking as a subject vis-à-vis an object.

The second fundamental difference is that Islamic philosophy is based on the image of a threefold human being consisting of body, soul and spirit. This means that the cognizing soul receives its impressions from two sides, the world of the senses and the world of the spirit. Philosophy without impressions from the spirit is not really possible, for philosophy means that human beings have the intrinsic need to orient themselves also on the spirit. This is really a longing to reconnect with God, the divine origin from which the human being has come forth.

Islamic philosophy is therefore in principle religious. Philosophy and theology are not separated. Realizing this is essential for an understanding of Iranian and Islamic philosophy.

CHAPTER 7

Thinking in the Light of the Spirit: Elements from Iranian Philosophy

Homage to Henry Corbin[213] *who opened the door to the world of Iranian thinking for me, and thanks to David Kuhrt who, in his "hermitage" near Forest Row, England, tirelessly "takes to heart" the works of Sohrawardi, Molla Sadra, Mehdi Hairi Yazdi and others, again and again giving me new leads.*

One day when I was traveling through Iran and was walking with a German-speaking friend around the great central square in Isfahan, I was addressed by a young Iranian. He had been reading a little book which I right away recognized as a publication of Reclam* because of its bright yellow color. It turned out to be *Der Ursprung des Kunstwerkes* (The Origin of the Work of Art) by Martin Heidegger. In faultless German he asked me to tell him the meaning of a German word, which I was unable to explain to him in Farsi. But we did have a brief conversation about philosophy and contemporary art. He was one of the hundreds of thousands of students of philosophy in Iran. Judging by the number of books appearing every year about western and eastern ways of thinking, Iran takes first place in the world as regards publications of philosophical texts. Studying philosophy is "in" in Iran, and in its long history this has always been the same.

---

* Translator's note: *Reclam* is a well-known German publisher.

Introduction: Self and Other

Something can only be other because there also is self. Everything that is other is in the first instance measured, or one could say tested, against and by the selfness of the one who does the measuring. Frequently, these are moments that are stamped forever in the memory: when for the first time the otherness of the other penetrates in full force into our consciousness, and brings about the awakening of self.

In the final analysis, other *comes into being* in this test. As a matter of fact, the test itself is the moment when both self and other come into being. Until that happens, the naïve premise may stay in force that everything else is identical with what you are yourself or, at any rate, is supposed to be identical. Once the test has been performed, different possibilities may present themselves. One of those is a growing openness and interest in other. This does not happen very easily. For the natural tendency is to have an outspoken interest in oneself, accompanied by a resistance to all that is not in harmony with its selfness. In the words of Oscar Wilde, "to love oneself" is the beginning of a lifelong love story.

Different strategies may be used here. Numerous forms of interest in other are merely disguises of interest in self. For instance, the interest in part of the western world in all that is eastern, called "orientalism" by Edward Said, ultimately consists of pursuing representations that serve one's own identity. Other then becomes an instrument for the fulfillment of one's own needs and requirements.

More subtle forms of a disguised interest in self are those in which one appreciates the other to the extent that it corresponds with self. In this way, thinkers from other cultures may be embraced in western culture when they express subjects such as emancipation, secularization and free speech in a way that is considered correct and expected in western culture. "They are part of us!" Such an embrace looks more like an appropriation. Other is then annexed into self, declared to be part of self, sometimes to the great surprise of the other!

In the worldwide debate going on between the world of western Christianity and that of Islam, vigilance is needed to discern all forms of—often unconscious and well-intended—appropriation, first of all regarding the view that all religions flow into one great, universal religion in which differences and contradictions cease to exist. It is a hopeful picture: all religions on the way to the same point where they will converge and where all points of view will be reconciled. However, religions and convictions cannot be on the way. Only people can be on the way. And there can be no question of being on the way together to this point of convergence. At best everyone is on the way as an individual, all by himself.

All speaking of a point where everything flows together into a higher unity, necessarily has to take place out of separate paths leading to this point. No one can walk all paths to this point at the same time. And precisely to the extent that someone is on the way he cannot claim to have a bird's eye view from a point above and beyond his specific position. Pointing to a point of convergence—assuming that it even exists—while everyone is still on the way, is premature and it infringes on the right to be other. At best one can indicate the way one is walking oneself.

That the way of another would lead to a point "where everything and everyone will come together" is an invalid idea. "They are also on the right path" is therefore an empty assertion. For it expresses the claim that one knows the destination of that path, a claim one can only make regarding one's own path. This does not deny the possibility of a point of convergence. How could we go on our way if at the horizon there were not something which beckons and calls us? However, no matter how much such a call seems to harbor an ideal of the future, pitfalls such as reductionism, standardization and appropriation are inevitable parts of it.

In this way, enthusiastic and well-intentioned Muslims have used some well-chosen quotations to call Goethe a self-declared Muslim. That does not mean that Goethe could under no circumstances have been a Muslim. The question at hand is rather: who is entitled to make such a statement?

What can preserve us from such pitfalls is the power to keep our balance between the longing that "all may come together in the one great house of the Father," and the daily practice of making one's lonely way through the dense "undergrowth of existence" where everything that surrounds us is other and, often painfully, forces itself onto us.

It becomes more difficult—because also more sensitive—when for instance someone uses Koran quotations to demonstrate that Muslims can also develop a relationship to Jesus, which needs not be all that different from our own relationship to Him. "They also know Jesus! They also have a Holy Spirit!" What unconsciously resounds then is something like "they are not so different after all, not so other, not so strange." But again the question is: who is entitled to make such a statement? From there the step to a pronouncement such as "Islam can also be understood as a form of Christianity" is not so farfetched. The next step is then the pitfall of appropriation.

The other way around, Mohammed Abduh[214] made the statement that Christianity, and in particular Protestantism, actually is more or less a form of Islam. Only, they are not yet aware of it. "The Christians' convictions differ from Islam only in the names they give them, not in spirit."

The inviolable otherness, the "foreignness" of Islam—and of every other religion or world view—must then be softened because there are also elements that can be called "Christian" or, the other way around, as in the case of Abduh. In my view this decidedly goes too far. Just like all other religions and cultures, Islam has the right to be inalienably other.

The misleading aspect of appropriation is that it invariably also has an element of truth to it. Yes indeed, Goethe had a deep connection both with the world of Islam and with the Persian culture, both before and after the rise of Islam. And yes, Muslims venerate Isa (Jesus) son of Maryam and word of God,[215] and acknowledge him as a prophet immediately after Mohammed in importance.

Not infrequently, appropriations indicate an authentic search for the uniqueness of the other, what is self in the other. If initial resistance and rejection of other can be transformed into interest, the risk of appropriation may be diminished, provided that after the phase of wonder and attraction—which may still contain a large portion of self-interest—the step can be made to acknowledging the actual otherness of other. The self of the other then reveals itself in its being other, foreign. This demands to be recognized, with all the feelings of powerlessness and bewilderment it will engender, coupled with the intention to persist and keep one's balance in this conflict. In other words, one way or the other there will be a conflict. As long as I experience other as "how interesting!" I have not yet perceived it in its true reality. For such perception is always frightening, alarming. Rilke wrote: "Every angel is terrifying."

Other is only other if it can be so, absolutely and radically. There is no such thing as "mitigating" being other, or "a little bit other." In the radically other I meet reality in the way Heidegger described it: standing in the storms of existence that pull and assail me from all sides. For this reason other demands an engagement that, in its radicalism, approaches what is radically other. If not, the danger is great that in numerous, sincerely well-intentioned attempts at dialog what is radically other will be lost. And because other cannot exist without self, self also will be lost.

THE PHILOSOPHY OF FREEDOM IN IRANIAN ISLAM

Philosophy in Iran

One of the many misunderstandings regarding Iranian culture is that it is presumed to be the same as Arabic culture. For instance, some surveys of Iranian culture continue to list Ibn Sina (Avicenna, 980-1037) among Arabic philosophers; also Al-Ghazali (1058-1111) and many others. This misunderstanding exists of course not only for Iranian philosophy. Literature and art are often treated likewise. In her highly commendable work about the inspiration which Goethe received for his collection of poems *West-Östliche Divan* ("West-Eastern Divan") from Hafez, an eminently Iranian classical poet, Katharina Mommsen, gave the first edition of this work the title "Goethe and the Arabic world!"[216]

What has contributed to this misunderstanding is the fact that many Iranian thinkers wrote a number of their works in Arabic, the scientific language of their time. However, it goes much deeper than the language. Iranian philosophy has an outspoken identity of its own and has a rich history that continues to unfold in our time. Seyyed Hossein Nasr, a contemporary Iranian philosopher, speaks of a "living philosophical tradition" and places Iranian philosophy within the whole of Islamic philosophy, to the extent that the latter can also be called living.

> Most readers in the West are probably still unaware of what "a living Islamic philosophical tradition" means. In the prevalent intellectual map of the Western world, Islamic philosophy is equated with that which the Latins called "Arabic philosophy" ... and identified with Latin Averroism, the disputations of St. Thomas and Duns Scotus or the arcane art of Raymondus Lullius. They hardly ever think of Islamic philosophy in later centuries.... The Islamic philosophical tradition is also a tradition which has continued to live until the present day especially in Iran. Suhrawardi and Ibn Sina and other Islamic philosophers are alive and belong to the present moment of the life of Persians and other Muslims in general, for whom the Islamic intellectual tradition is "alive." Unfortunately most Western scholars of Islam have not appreciated this fact and in their studies and analyses of Islamic civilization ... have until recently cut off their discussions with the sixth/twelfth or seventh/thirteenth centuries. In most cultural studies and those dealing with intellectual history all the later phases of Islamic philosophy, Sufism and theology, as well as astronomy, mathematics and medicine are neglected almost systematically.[217]

High Points

In a continuous line, from the proclamations of Zarathustra and philosophical treatises of his revelations, via the great systems of Mani (third century CE) and Mazdak (fifth century CE) to the first instructions of the Imams (from the seventh century) and Ishmaelite schools, and the high points of Avicenna (Ibn Sina), Ghazali, Sohrawardi, Molla Sadra—without interruption, thinking in the Iranian world revolves around the idea of the spirit and its essence, and the way it affects the world.

Parallel to this we witness the philosophical and scientific analysis of the legacy of ancient Hellenistic thought in many universities, which continues in a never-ending discussion in Iran even into our days. In the following we will present three high points in this thinking of the spirit.

A first high point is that of Avicenna (980-1037), the founder of an ontology that forms a unique synthesis of Neoplatonic and Aristotelian metaphysics; this makes it possible to attribute an individualizing role to the soul as the mediating principle between body and spirit.[218] Closely following Avicenna's footsteps comes Sohrawardi (1155-1191) who, building on the emanation doctrine of Avicenna, designs a synthesis of the pre-Islamic light doctrine from the Zarathustra tradition and an epistemology that is based on the thinking of the spirit. Independent of these developments stands the great Andalusian Ibn Arabi (1165-1240), in whose thinking the transcendent unity of being and the cognition* thereof converge, and who creates a systematic terminology of mystical experience that even today is fundamental to theology, mysticism, psychology and philosophy in the world of Islam. Ibn Arabi exceeds the framework of Iranian theology and philosophy.

A second high point is Molla Sadra (1571-1641),[219] who in his turn will form a synthesis of the triumvirate Avicenna, Sohrawardi and Ibn Arabi and a thinking of the spirit in which the contrast between mystical insight and conceptual thinking is overcome. One could also call it an enlightened thinking which in its very essence includes religious experience. Just like his great predecessors, Molla Sadra pays great attention to the realm of images, a world between the dimension of the physical and that of the spirit, which is accessible to thinking, provided that thinking is able to free itself from rigid concepts and comes to life again. The philosophy of Molla Sadra is not a closed system, but it invites one to participate in a further search for

---

* Translator's note: I have attempted, not always successfully depending on the context, to maintain a distinction between *cognition* as the act of knowing, and *knowledge* as the result of the act of knowing.

a bridge between transcendent unity and the multiplicity of the created world. That his thinking continues to be of eminent importance is indicated by the fact that Molla Sadra's work is still the foundation of the study of philosophy in Iran. The University of Tehran has a special chair dedicated to the study of his thought.

A third high point is the philosophy of Mehdi Hairi Yazdi (1923-1999),[220] who aims to create a synthesis of western epistemology and the thinking of the spirit in the context of the Iranian tradition. Yazdi, who taught philosophy at the University of Tehran, certainly had epistemology in mind. However, it is not about a knowledge that consists in collecting, analyzing, and relating data. He spoke of a process of cognition in which the thinker must necessarily be involved in order for knowledge to be able to exist. Yazdi called this "knowledge by presence." But his intention was the exact description and representation of all the elements that characterize this cognition by presence. As a thinker in the twentieth century, Yazdi was able to draw on a philosophical and intellectual tradition of more than a thousand years in Iran. His great sources of inspiration were Avicenna, Sohrawardi and Molla Sadra. The extraordinary aspect of Yazdi is that he entered into dialog with westerners such as Kant, James, Wittgenstein and Russell and tried to find concurrences between these and Iranian philosophers.

Iranian culture as a whole was confronted not just once, but twice, with the phenomenon of prophecy and the revelations it generated. The first time was with the revelations and teaching of Zarathustra, who has deep roots in Iranian identity; then came the revelations and teaching of Mohammed, which struck wounds in this Iranian self-consciousness, but also created a climate in which Shiism could flourish. The question of the knowability of the supreme reality—God—and the dynamism of His self-revelation through a prophet was born from this double influence. Even today this question is still haunting Iranian thinking.

It is not a simple thing to place this type of thinking in one of the categories of western thinking. One can call it theology, or theosophy, philosophy, metaphysics, ontology—it is all of these, and yet none of these fully cover it. It is at any rate a type of thinking that includes experience, without for that reason being gnosis in the usual sense of the word. It is a thinking which imposes on itself a strict discipline of laying a foundation of rationality and systematic exploration, but it is not *kalām*.[221*]

---

* Translator's note: The *Kalām* cosmological argument is a variation of the cosmological argument that argues for the existence of a first cause for the universe, and the existence of a god. Its origins can be traced to medieval Jewish, Christian and Muslim thinkers, but most directly to Islamic theologians of the Kalām tradition. (Source: Wikipedia)

To the extent that it leads to schools it exists *within* and not *outside* the established religious order. It often has a tense relationship with the religious establishment and can similarly also develop conflicts with the political powers. But it has an unmistakable place of its own within the whole of Iranian culture, also in our time. The representatives of this thinking include both clerics and seculars and they teach both at universities and in religious schools—both sectors of society participate in this process. But it may just as well exist outside of these sectors. And it too is a continuous fixture of thinking in the Iranian world: the unmistakable presence of philosophical debate in public discourse, which expands the horizon of the public forum so that it extends far beyond the events that are currently happening.

Every thinker, irrespective of when he lived, to the extent that he is present and brings his voice into the debate, contributes to its timeliness. The concept of the history of philosophy does not correspond with its western interpretation. There is no modern or post-modern philosophy. There is a thinking that moves to the center—the thinking of the spirit as reality—and there is a thinking that remains at the periphery. The questions that arise here, such as the relationship between thinking and revelation, are just as valid in the twenty-first century as they were in the time when Avicenna and Ghazali were living.

Philosophy in the world of Islam cannot be reduced to a philosophical school or academic orientation, for it is a discipline which also brings with it an inner transformation. Sohrawardi called the way of the philosopher a way that leads to spiritual and moral perfection. This path leads to a synergy between discerning reason, cognitive enlightenment in the soul, and intuition of reality in the spirit.

General Characteristics of Islamic Philosophy

It might be interesting to see whether it would be possible to speak of a history of philosophy in the Islamic world the way we do in the West, where we view the history of philosophy as the story of transformations and new paradigms that develop through the centuries, such as the leap from scholasticism with its integral way of thinking to the Cartesian paradigm with its split between subject and object.[222]

In Islam the case is rather that from the beginning we see the development of different circles, or schools, and these circles continue to exist into our time. We run a big risk if we would view this as a kind of stagnation. That would be completely incorrect. In the West the differences show up one after the other; in the world of

Islam they exist one beside the other. Over time, the West has developed more and more emphasis on the causal linearity of history, namely that the later comes into being out of the earlier, and coupled with this, an overvaluation of the most recent.

While, beginning in the seventeenth century, western philosophy becomes characterized by modernity and the subject-object split, with all the centrifugal forces it generates even today,[223] this is not at all the case for the whole of Islamic philosophy. When in the history of western philosophy, from the beginning of modern times, the questions become more and more specialized, with ever sharper distinctions between philosophy, science and theology, thinking will diverge more and more into different directions and *become farther and farther removed from the center.*

By contrast, thinking in the Islamic world *moves to a center.* In the center stand the question of being and the potential of the human being to achieve cognition of being. This highest Being, which is its own cause, is at the same time essence and, as such, truth and reality in their purest state. This is expressed by the word *haqiqat.*[224]

This center is not a static place but a dynamic center. The highest Being which forms the center in the center, the highest form of Being (God), generates out of itself the movement of its revelation. God communicates Himself, and these communications travel to the world of human beings where they are ultimately reflected in word and writing. The Book, the holy Koran, is the reflection of this self-revealing communication of the deepest reality, which is in God and is God. In the world of Islam, research into thinking is therefore characterized by hermeneutics of the revelation and the modalities of its cognition, i.e., the different ways to penetrate to this deepest reality. If thinking also includes finding a relationship to what exists, in the center of all that *is* stands the revealed Book; and it is one of the tasks of thinking to find a relationship in truth to the revealed Book.

The Principal Spheres of Activity of Philosophy

Falsafa

Falsafa is simply the Arab word for philosophy. And yet it is not the same as philosophy in the broad sense of the word—it only applies to the philosophy that was handed down in the traditions of the Greek-Roman and Indo-Iranian heritage; those schools therefore where the wisdom of antiquity is studied and developed further. This encompasses all branches of philosophy and science that existed in the scriptures available in Hellenistically inspired academies both in the Byzantine and Persian empires. Galenus, Ptolemaeus, the Stoa, Plato and the Neo-Platonists, Aristotle and Theophrastus all play important roles here. Although explored to a lesser extent, Indian and Persian thinking have also played important roles in the transfer of knowledge between different disciplines and cultures.

Besides interpretation and commentary, the most important fields of activity in this school are philology (for instance, the comparison of different translations) and study. It is important that the ancient sciences, the *ulum al-awa'il*, are not simply adopted, but are taken a step further and even transformed! The central question is to what extent the instruments of cognition of ancient philosophy, such as logic and intellectually developed proof, are able to contribute to a thinking penetration of revelation.

Kalam

Kalam means "word" or "logos," "discourse"; it is a practice of dialectic theology, which means that on the basis of logical argumentation, with the word therefore, the revealed truths are interpreted and, if necessary, defended. This frequently happened in the form of a public debate in which different points of view would collide in this way. Part of this school is the creation of law, i.e., the thinking exegesis of normative law from the Koran and the *hadith*, which freely developed into the ninth century and was thereafter further applied in the existing schools of law.

Within Sunni Islam four great schools of law have developed, and within Shiite Islam a fifth. One of the great representatives of *kalam* in the Shiite context was Nasiroddin Tusi (1201-1274). Islamic law (*fiqh*) is derived from the Koran and *hadith*, and is further developed on the basis of consensus and reasoning by analogy. Generally it is said that the development of principles of law on the basis of logic, called *ijtihad*, stopped at the end of the tenth century. This is expressed in the phrase "the closing of the gates of *ijtihad*." There is no agreement as to precisely when this happened, and it is a question whether this happened for all schools of law at the same time and in the same way, especially in the case of the Shiite school of law.

Theology or *Hikmat Ilahya*

Hikma means "wisdom" and the expression *hikmat ilahya* actually means "theosophy" and can be used in the sense of either "divine wisdom" or "wisdom of the divine." Sometimes the term *hikma* is replaced by *ilm*—science, scholarship. *Ilm ilahya* comes closer to the western meaning of the word theology, study of God.

This goes deeper than just a different nuance. *Hikmat ilahya* emphasizes the thinking-experiencing exploration of the phenomenon of revelation and prophecy;

ilm ilahya focuses on what was revealed, the Book, which in turn is put in practice in the science of law, *al fiqh*. Here we see frequent points of interface with *kalam*, especially when in the course of discursive argumentation the methods of reasoning from Greek science are invoked.

Nevertheless, the thinking experience of the reality of God's word is not gnosis, nor is it a mystical experience. The thinking penetration of the differences, the layers of meaning of the Koran, remains an exercise of the human spirit and, particularly when the emphasis is on scholarship, the methodology of logical argumentation and arriving at proof is an obvious instrument.

Intuitive Cognition or *Hikmat 'Irfani*

'Irfan means "insight" and in a specific context, e.g., in the further development of Iranian philosophy starting with Sohrawardi (1155-1191),[225] it could also mean "gnosis," inner insight. It refers to the form of cognition in which thinking no longer needs the support of what is given but is capable of carrying itself, which generates a process of inner revelation. The literal word as revealed in the Koran is no longer the only object of exploration, even though every spiritual search begins first with revelation, but it is at the same time a medium to penetrate to an experience of the spiritual as unmediated cognition. However, this experience is a continuation of the process of thinking.

In the Iranian philosophical tradition this form of cognition is also called *ishraqi*. Literally this means "(rising in) the East" or "eastern," but it is also often translated as "illuminative cognition" because at the moment when intuitive cognition reveals itself in the soul it may be compared with the rising of the sun.

For clarification it must be noted that these four large domains, in which many additional nuances may be distinguished and in which thinking moves in the world of Islam, must not be viewed as four separate areas. Numerous thinkers have worked in at least two or three of these areas, which does not preclude that they have excelled in one of them. The greatest among them, such as Sohrawardi, Ibn Arabi and Molla Sadra, achieved a degree of perfection in all four, which enabled them to create in themselves a level of integration of these four and thus lay the foundation for renewal. It is precisely this capacity that makes them unique. This does not diminish the intrinsic value of thinkers and scholars such as Omar Khayyam and Rumi.

The Freedom Impulse in Islam

Duty and Right

In the centuries during which Islamic philosophy has developed, freedom has been a theme that has been investigated in Islamic thinking. The questions this has raised are fundamentally different from those that have become paramount in western thinking ever since the age of Enlightenment. In current western culture, religion and freedom exclude each other, or tradition and secularism exclude each other. Abdolkarim Soroush, a contemporary Iranian philosopher, characterizes it as follows:

> In its new world view (since the age of Enlightenment) modern humanity has developed a new relationship with religion…. A modern human being is critical and demanding (not impassive and peaceful); he looks for changes (not just understanding);… he is active (not passive); he is familiar with skepticism and uncertainty (not with certainty); he is interested in clarity and causality (not in perplexity and enchantment); he likes to show off and enjoy (does not regret separation); he is conscious of life (not of death); he pursues rights (not only duties);… he intervenes in life (is not just a consumer of life); he uses reason in service of critique (not only for understanding). Modern humanity is unconscious of its limitations and proud of its creative potential. For this reason it is far removed from Rumi's description: "Since we are the created rather than the Creator, we are expected to be gentle and modest."[226]

However, it is certainly not Soroush's intention to trade modernity for a return to tradition. He searches for the point where religion and secularism converge and cease to exclude each other by definition. A government is only an instrument, and it can only interpret that which sets the tone in a society. Consequently, a government cannot be religious; only a society, a totality of people who form part of a state, can be religious, says Soroush in the same article.

In regard to the subject of freedom he makes a distinction between tradition, in which duties regulate society, and a secular society, in which individual rights are the criterion. Secularism means that a change is made in the relationship between duty and right. Duty, according to Soroush, is the task of respecting the rights of the other, even at the cost of one's own interests. The duty of husband and wife is to observe each other's rights, which are in this case not identical but express the differences in their tasks within the family and within the totality of society.

In a discussion after a lecture on freedom and rights, a Muslim woman stated her views as follows: "I am not forced (by law) to make a voluntary contribution. Yet, it is my duty." Namely the duty to observe the rights of the other, in this case, the right to receive the necessities of life. Sharia is about the duties which are part of the task of each human being, namely the duty to respect and observe the rights of the other.

Western secular society is concerned first of all with the right that is *my* due, not the right of *the other*. If this right is interfered with, I can insist on it for myself through the law.

"In my opinion," writes Soroush, "this is one of the principal reasons why the modern world cannot understand the principles of an Islamic government."[227] For an Islamic government the fundamental principle is that of duty. Duty and freedom do not exclude each other. I can decide in freedom to respect the rights of the other. Duty does not need to be obligation. Obligation is in a certain sense a reduction of this basic principle which, however, runs counter to the basic principles of a secular form of government, where the principles of human rights are fundamental. But here a reduction is also possible. I can pursue the right that is my due within society at the expense of the other.

Seyyed Hossein Nasr speaks in this connection of the difference between the "pontifical" person and the "promethean" person. The pontifical person is the one who builds a bridge in his thinking and actions between the divine order and the human order. He shows a sense for cohesion. Prometheus is the one who through guile brought fire from the divine world to the human world. His way begins with a disruption of the existing order.[228]

The Idea of Freedom

Philosophically speaking, freedom is a subject which, in one way or another, appears again and again within the context of the central themes in Islamic thinking: God as self-creating being, His knowledge of Himself, His knowledge of the creatures who have their origin in His being; and the human being as *khalifah*, His representative on earth. What in western philosophy in the Middle Ages became the question of divine providence in relation to the will (free or unfree) of the human being is in Islamic thought the question whether God, in His knowledge of His own being, at the same time also knows the beings He created, in the same way in which He knows Himself.

God, as the cause of all that exists, cannot but know that which has arisen through Him. But how can this knowledge be defined? Is it a knowledge of the particular, or is it universal knowledge? But how can we comprehend that the particular can be an object of knowledge for divine cognition which is all-encompassing? In the terminology of Avicenna and others: is God's knowledge a knowledge of the essentials or, at the same time, a knowledge of the particular or of the accidentals? Knowledge of the essentials refers to eternal and unchangeable being. It is outside the dimensions of space and time. The particular, however, means movement, and therefore change, and it exists in the sub-lunar world, the world in which we live. If God, in his self-contemplation, also knows all possible changes, we stand before the problem of predestination. Did God know all possible changes from all eternity? In that case, the human being does not have free will. And if divine knowledge only encompasses the essentials, then His knowledge—and thus His being—is imperfect. On this point the question is not just about human free will, but likewise about whether God in his self-contemplation, which is an activity, arrives at all-encompassing cognition.

The presumption of God's all-encompassing knowledge, while yet allowing for changes of the particular in the sub-lunar sphere, has brought many thinkers to wide detours, if not to an impasse. For instance, with the aid of logical arguments, Avicenna finally arrives at the conclusion that God has knowledge of a moon eclipse, which takes place in space and time, and also that He has knowledge of whether or not Socrates will drink the cup of poison. Except that in the latter case it is less evident than with the moon eclipse! God has knowledge of the possibility of drinking the cup of poison or not doing so, and of the fact that drinking it is a deed oriented toward the good, more so than not drinking it. God also has knowledge of Socrates' essence (the nature of his being) which is oriented toward the good.[229] However, this does not mean that Socrates' deed was predestined. God's knowledge of Socrates' nature does not determine how the latter will give form to this nature.

This subtle distinction can easily be overlooked and lead to a view in which all human actions are preordained from all eternity. According to Avicenna, however, God's knowledge is that of the universals, not of the particular. This leaves open the possibility of freedom. In his commentary on *De Anima* by Aristotle he sees this reflected in the organization of human knowledge. There exists a cognition oriented to the general (theoretical knowing—*theory* here in its original meaning of the Greek *theorein*, to behold) and a cognition that is oriented to the particular (practical knowing, knowing that leads to action). For instance, theoretical knowledge allows us to have an overview of the totality of causes, in other words, to "behold" causality as a universal concept. Practical knowledge, on the other hand, can see only one cause for each concrete case. The possibility of freedom lies in the capacity to connect both forms of knowledge. Avicenna calls the transition between both forms the capacity of "imagination." In this region one finds oneself between the world of the created and the world of the creating origin. This *mundus imaginalis* is the area of transition between what is purely spiritual, all-encompassing being and that which has taken on a particular form in matter and is thus determined.

However, if one is unable to move between these two worlds, then the field of cognition remains limited to that of the particular, and rules of law and forms of organization are needed to regulate life. This is the meaning and significance of the directions which determine the relationships among the members of a community.[230]

Those, however, who through education, study and inner training prove to be capable of practicing these two modes of cognition have the right to practice jurisprudence independently on the basis of interpretation of the Koran and *hadith (ijtihad)*. This is especially true for the Shiite Safari school of law and, to a certain extent, also for the remaining four schools of law. In the tenth century of the Christian age, however, the gates of *ijtihad* were closed. This means that new interpretations may still be arrived at, but no new rules of law may be added to the already existing body of law.[231]

The expression *ijtihad* is based on the root j-h-d, in which one can easily recognize the word *jihad*. Here, however, in the sense meant above, the great *jihad* is meant, the struggle in one's own soul in order to open the soul to knowledge through imagination. In tradition this struggle was called the "polishing of the mirror of the soul." Both Al-Ghazali (see below) and Avicenna have written about it. Some of their reflections on this can be found at the end of this contribution.

Avicenna: Soul and Body—A New Element

> Komayl ibn Zyad, pupil of Ali ibn Talib, first Imam and son-in-law of Mohammed, asks Ali:
> "Master, speak to me about my soul. Teach me to know my soul!"
> To which Ali replies:
> "Which soul do you wish me to teach you to know?"
> "Master, is then the soul not one and the same in its being?"
> "Struggling against the soul through knowledge is the mark of the intellect."[232]

Avicenna[233] was one of the very first scholars in the eleventh century who had at his disposal the virtually complete body of the works of Plato, Aristotle and their successors. Highly gifted, he absorbed these texts already at a very young age, and then developed his own original thinking out of them. His thorough knowledge of the state of science and philosophy of his time enabled him to develop a synthesis quite his own. A great deal is known of his life, such as his early fame as a physician (he was seventeen when he succeeded in healing the Samani prince Nuh al-Mansur!), his wanderings in the footsteps of local rulers to whom he offered his services in exchange for access to their libraries, his public functions by day and his philosophical work at night, his freewheeling lifestyle—all of this would make him into a legendary figure.

Much of his work, including the 20-volume *Kitab al-Insaf*, was irretrievably lost due to chaotic events even during his life. However, his thinking went into a new direction and formed a basis for other philosophers to develop their own thinking of the spirit.

Al Ghazali made a deep study of Avicenna's work. The notion that he became an opponent of philosophy on the basis of Avicenna's work, with the result that he brought the "golden period of philosophy and science" to an end, is a misconception. This view goes back to some interpretations by the orientalist Ignaz Goldziher (1850-1921) and conclusions therefrom. In a recent study of Avicenna and his philosophical legacy this view, which is widespread in the West, is revised. Al-Ghazali found room for a number of important teachings of Greek-oriented philosophers within the constellation of the Islamic faith,[234] and the work of Avicenna formed the basis for that of subsequent generations of theologians and philosophers.

A revolution in thinking. Avicenna's first but certainly not his only great contribution to the rebirth of thinking in the Iranian world is his doctrine of the soul in relation to body and spirit. Well acquainted with *De Anima* by Aristotle and his terminology, he restored to the soul its role and significance. In his *Kitab al-Nafs* ("Book on the Soul") he added new elements to thinking about the soul, albeit in the light of Plato and Aristotle. *Kitab al-Nafs* forms part of an encyclopedic work entitled *Shifa* ("Book of Healing") which encompasses logic, physics and metaphysics.

While in faculties of science and medicine, such as in Gondishapur, the exegesis of Aristotle continued to be practiced along the lines of a then age-old tradition, Avicenna laid the foundation for a new teaching of the soul, and he can be viewed as the founder of thinking of the spirit.

Truly revolutionary was his thesis that it is not the body that individualizes, as was Aristotle's view, but the soul which sets its own unique stamp on the as yet undetermined physical disposition. While in the extreme western part of the Islamic world this basic Aristotelian principle placed Averroes before a near unsolvable philosophical-theological problem, in the Iranian-Islamic world a totally different path was found a century before Averroes. The principle of individualization is attributed to the soul. Not only does this guarantee the unity of human nature, but also its unicity! The surprising thing is that, in order to explain this "revolution" that it is the soul which individualizes, Avicenna develops a cosmology of which the key principle is active thinking itself. He does this by building further on what his great predecessor and compatriot Al-Farabi had developed, namely the distinction between *Being*, which by its nature necessarily engenders itself, and *being* which, due to its nature, is necessarily engendered by another. This distinction of two great categories of being was invaluable for the further deployment of thinking in Iran and in the world of Islam in general.

The doctrine of emanation. The first category is the highest Being. God is *Being* which generates itself and in which disposition and realization ceaselessly bring each other into movement in a process of self-realization.

The second category encompasses the many *beings* that have been called into existence by the highest Being, including the human being. Human beings, however, are placed in the noteworthy situation that they are able to think this highest Being, which in itself is the cause of all things. This means that the human being cannot be placed on the same level as all other beings.

This fundamental distinction between Being which *has generated itself* and all being which *was generated by Being* is the ground on which all further thinking of the Spirit will firmly stand.

This leads Avicenna to design a doctrine of emanation in which the highest Being in self-realization necessarily contemplates itself and completely knows itself. This self-contemplation, which one may also call absolute self-knowledge, is total and completely transparent because there is no element in its being which has not been generated by Being itself. It is the self-contemplation of the highest Being that now generates the first being, a being that owes its existence to another outside itself. However, this first being is still so fully filled with this capacity of self-contemplation that it is able to generate in its own thinking a subsequent being; and this goes on to the tenth being, which, while still capable of thinking itself in total clarity, is no longer able to generate a new being.

This succession of ten beings—the first, highest Being and the nine subsequent beings—represent in their order of rank the totality of the angelic hierarchies. In Islamic tradition, the angelic hierarchies were created by God before he proceeded to create the human being. When one now approaches this in active thinking, it means that the highest Being in self-knowledge (contemplation of self), which is none other than presence to and in Himself, generates out of this overfullness other beings who, in contrast with the human being, continue to embody a unity of disposition and realization. The tenth and last in this ranking is called the Angel of Revelation or the Angel of Annunciation. It is none other than the angel Gabriel of Christian tradition.

Avicenna is unique in that he developed an epistemology that is both angelology and anthropology.

The twofold dynamic of love. Among these ranks of beings moves a twofold dynamic, a descending and an ascending movement between the highest Being and the world of humans. Avicenna describes this in terminology that comes close to Neo-Platonism: he speaks of love which, on the one hand, rises like a stream from the lowest to the highest ranks of beings and, on the other hand, also descends from the highest to the lowest. In this way the higher awakens in the lower what is its "germ of development," the longing to ascend.

The revolutionary aspect of his thinking lies in the way Avicenna connected this with the dynamic in body, soul and spirit in the human being. At this point angelology is transformed into anthropology. In human beings love is also the motive that awakens a longing in them to develop themselves. The soul plays a central role in this. Vis-à-vis the body the soul represents the higher, but vis-à-vis the spirit it represents the lower.

It is love which stimulates the soul, as the higher with respect to the body, to individualize the body. This longing for self-realization makes a unique imprint: it makes the human being into a unique individual. And it is the same dynamic that causes the soul to open itself to the cognizing spirit, the higher. In its turn, the soul receives the stamp of the spirit and can then, in its mediating function, imprint this onto the body. All human beings carry in themselves the potential to realize themselves through the same dynamic that also ascends and descends through the hierarchies of angels. The soul has the key role here. Without its mediation, and without its movement to the lower as well as to the higher in itself, no individualization will take place. In different words: whether this potential is realized depends on the soul.

The as yet neutral form principle, the *causa formalis* of Aristotle, now explicitly receives love as its motive force. It is love which induces the form principle to unite with *hyle*, the principle of matter. And conversely, the soul will make itself receptive in the way in which the body is receptive to it. In this movement to the higher the *intellectus agens*, which is the Angel of Revelation, can, as the higher relative to itself, unite with the soul out of love. Thus the soul, in its turn, achieves self-knowledge. It knows itself as it is in reality: forming in regard to the body, receiving in regard to the spiritual. This does demand a willingness to turn inward, to "return to and into itself." This turning inward is miles removed from any narcissistic self-involvement. Contemplation of self means knowledge of self. For the soul, self-knowledge is the realization of its higher nature. Then the soul becomes the "soul which has come to rest in itself" and is able to achieve this transformation, which consists of contemplation of its own essence. This enables the soul to fulfill the task it is given in the Koran:

> O soul that art at rest! Return to your Lord, well-pleased (with Him), well-pleasing (Him).[235]

The moment of the Holy Spirit. Here we come to an important principle in the philosophy of the Spirit, as developed by Avicenna, that the higher can only connect itself with the lower if the lower is willing to receive the higher. The dynamic of love must work in both directions. If this creative penetration by the higher into the lower through the ten ranks of emanation can be understood as a process of unfolding of the highest Being who, overflowing with creative power, shares his Being downward from rank to rank, then this ceases at the tenth rank, the rank of the Angel of Revelation. Below this stands the human being, and the process of creative sharing can only continue if there exists a willingness to be receptive in the human soul, the place where, according to Avicenna, it is the human being's first and, one could say, natural tendency to create forms for impressions received through the senses.

The activation of the faculty of cognition is none other than the change that makes the soul receptive to the influence of the tenth Intelligence or the Angel of Revelation. This being awakens forms of cognition in the now receptive soul, forms of cognition that are no longer derived from the sense world. This enables the soul to perfect itself in such a way that it becomes able to have insight into its own being. It is this growing self-knowledge, the increasing transparency of the soul, that individualizes the human being. The Intelligence which awakens the forms of cognition is separated—fully in the Aristotelian sense.

This process of cognition brings about something in the soul, namely that the soul becomes present to itself, something that was not there before and now becomes a kernel of individualization. There is a moment in this process when the receptive and self-observing soul becomes intimately united with the active influence of the tenth Intelligence, which is the Holy Spirit. Avicenna understands this moment in all its intimacy as the decisive moment when the totality of the ranks of autonomous Intelligences, which came into existence out of the highest Being, are "present in the soul." It is a sacred moment, a moment of becoming whole. Does not the soul heal itself as its self-knowledge grows? Therefore, this moment is called the moment of the Holy Spirit, *al-Ruh al-Quds* or *'Aql Qodsi*. For this reason, the document in which the "healer" Avicenna wrote this down has the title *The Book of Healing*.

This moment of holiness/wholeness that is consummated between soul and spirit must be considered as an exception. Not everyone is able to achieve it. But what has been given to everyone is the immediate (i.e., without any intermediary) awareness of being a self, in the sense that there is a pre-conscious knowing that "this am I," a pre-conscious form of presence to oneself. Thus Avicenna is speaking of a knowing that is never interrupted and that he views as the prerequisite for the return into oneself after the accomplished deed of cognition, in which this pre-conscious nature now becomes a conscious reality.

Contemplation as introspection and return to oneself. Thus there is a pre-conscious knowing of self *before* the deed of cognition (*al-shu'ur bi-l-thab*), a becoming aware of self *in* the act of cognition, and a consciousness of being self *after* the act of cognition as a return of the soul into itself (*al-shu'ur bi-l-iktisab*).

Only the soul is essential and determinative for the essence of individuality. But it also integrates, for it takes the previous moments of the act of cognition into itself in order to unite them in itself. In other words, self-knowledge becomes attainment (*al-shu'ur bi-l-shu'ur*). A sharp distinction is made here between pre-conscious self and individuality attained in consciousness. If there is continued existence of the soul, this only applies to the soul which, in the process of achieving the deed of cognition, perceives itself, understands, observes and knows itself.

Avicenna clearly shows in the trilogy of mystical works he has written that this thinking also includes experience. There he gives us a glimpse of his own path of the return of the soul to and into itself.[236] He called his own most personal philosophy *Hikmat Mashriqiyya* (Wisdom of the East). This "East" has nothing to do with the orientalism that was challenged by Edward Said, nor with any vague enthusiasm and wishful thinking around a sentimental picture of a distant and mysterious Orient. We will discover it in one of Avicenna's great successors, Sohrawardi, who was also the founder of the *Ishraqiyyun*, "they who think in the light of the rising sun."

In contrast with Averroes, whose thinking did not resonate much in the further development of Islamic philosophy, that of Avicenna has been the impulse to a mighty synthesis and long-lasting high point in thinking, to which numerous thinkers have contributed in the centuries that followed. We must not limit these to the Iranian world. One of them is Ibn Arabi, the "Shaykh al Akbar," the greatest among the masters, who, with his unsurpassed power to knit thinking together, to think in interconnectedness—the faculty to take seemingly divergent views, bring them together under the same denominator and thus connect them together in thinking on a higher level—has guided this stream, which arose from Avicenna, into broad further channels.[237] Those readers who would like to have an overview of this are referred to the entire work of Henry Corbin, the French Islam expert and orientalist whose life work consists, besides translating and publishing basic texts, in mapping these philosophical currents.

Sohrawardi: Thinking as Epiphany

On July 29, 1191,[238] seven years before Averroes, Shihaboddin Yahya Sohrawardi, born in northwest Iran, died in captivity in Aleppo. He was barely 36 years old. There is a strong suspicion that he was executed. His close connection with Al Malik al Zahir, son of Saladin (1137-1193), was a thorn in the side of the *ulemas*[*] who conducted a furious campaign against Sohrawardi and had accused him before Saladin of heresy and perversion of Malik. For this reason, he is regarded by many as a *shahid*—a witness, a martyr. His best known work, *Hikmat al-Ishraq* ("Wisdom of the East"), is a summit in which he unfolds all the wisdom he had acquired in one great panorama. The uniqueness of this work is that he also incorporates the wisdom teaching of Zarathustra and its further developments and, in so doing, rejuvenates Zarathustra's wisdom and gives it new spiritual power. Thus Iran sees for the first time a mighty integration of the foundational elements of its original culture, the prophet Zarathustra and his preaching, and the prophetic thinking of the Revelation as inspired by the Koran. And between these two pillars he weaves the thinking of Hellenistic philosophy and hermetic gnosis.

---

* Translator's note: Muslim scholars trained in Islam and Islamic law. (Source: American Heritage Dictionary)

In Sohrawardi's writings Zarathustra, Hermes and Plato enter into dialog with each other in a way that in the West took place only once, namely in the Academy of Florence[239] with Gemisthos Plethon in the company of Marsilio Ficino and Pico della Mirandola.

Light and darkness. In all of Sohrawardi's work we hear the ground tone of Iranian thinking, namely that wherever there is light, darkness reigns also. The two creative principles, Light and Darkness, proclaimed by Zarathustra as the primal principles of all that comes into being in time, Sohrawardi places in the process of human thinking itself. For thinking is also a process through time! After all, cognition—as an activity of the spirit—can exist only if the soul is ready to receive. There Sohrawardi follows the footsteps of Avicenna, when he describes the soul as the place where the dynamic between activity and receptivity is played out, between striving for form and longing to receive. When this longing becomes strong enough, the light of thinking can begin to shine in the soul, however, not *from outside inward* as in Aristotle and Averroes, but *from the inside out!* Thinking, which is light, makes its appearance in the soul just like the sun rising over the horizon. It lights up in the soul and this lighting up is at the same time a resurrection process taking place in the soul. For in this lighting up the true essence of cognition is revealed. It is Being which becomes present to itself in the act of cognition. It is disclosure (*kashf*) and presence (*hodur*) in one. In the moment of cognition the soul recognizes this essence as its own; in the soul, cognition makes itself known through its light and, because of this, it reveals to the soul the soul's own being. And in this moment it becomes true. Cognition, recognition and realization coincide. This is what is meant with the word *Ishraq*, the East, when Sohrawardi speaks of the Wisdom of the East; the school that arose from this is called the *'Ishraqiyyun*, "those who dwell in the East," meaning the region of revelation in the soul.

Light and darkness in the soul. Sohrawardi's exploration is directed to the phenomenon of this appearing, and to the region where it appears. That thinking is light is not a metaphor, even though it can be used in that way. Thinking is *truly* light. This means that it is the communication of being by the autonomous beings who form part of the Pleroma, the ten ranks of Intelligences which have been called into being by the self-communication of the highest Being, as described by Avicenna. Their essence is not the light, but the *communication of their essence* is light. It is *epiphany*. It is this communication in the soul, that is prepared for cognition, which makes its appearance like a sunrise. In the light of this sunrise the soul acknowledges itself and, in its turn, becomes communication. It communicates itself to itself. At the same time this is also a struggle, for a part of the soul resists this appearance of the light, just as the night fights the day. Sohrawardi gives all his attention, not to the tenth Intelligence (see Avicenna), but to the First who was created, which he calls by the Old-Persian name of *Vohu Manah*.[240]

Vohu Manah means "Good Spirit." The Old-Persian word *manah* is directly derived from the Sanskrit *manas*. Vohu Manah—called Vahman or Bahman in Middle-Persian, the language of the Sassanids—is the highest among the created Light Beings and reigns over the entire light world. Above him extends the world of the pure Spirit (*Ruhabad*), the Spirit to the extent that it does not (yet) communicate itself. At the other pole lies the world of pure matter, Darkness, indicated by Sohrawardi with the term *Barzakh*, literally meaning a "place of passage," "isthmus," but also "interval" and "disguise." But it is also an autonomous world, and in this sense Ruhabad and Barzakh are each other's direct opposites.

Gnostic influences. It is perfectly clear that we can here recognize Gnostic patterns and certain tendencies from Manichaeism, but also Mazdeic doctrine[241] which states that all that exists in the sense world (*getik*) has its counterpart in the supersensible world (*menok*). Both of these, *getik* and *menok*, have their place in the whole of Sohrawardi's teaching of the Spirit and the Pleroma of the Light Beings. In the world of *getik*, beings achieve their most condensed form and become impenetrable to the Light Beings, with the result that they become part of Darkness. In the world of *menok*, on the other hand, they are in a state of transparency to the Light Beings; they are "enlightened."

Sohrawardi identifies the light that thus announces itself in the inmost human being with the *Xvarna*,[242] the radiant royal luster as proclaimed by Zarathustra in his *Gathas*.[243] The moment of epiphany of the lighting up of the light of thinking in the soul coincides with the appearance of *Xvarna*, who is for the soul what the *Xvarna* as World Saviour (nineteenth Gatha) will be for humanity.

Between the pure spirit world on the one hand and the world of pure darkness on the other, regions develop which each take a well-determined position vis-à-vis the two extreme poles. These regions are quite decisive for the further thinking of the Spirit because Being works into them, and they can therefore create a picture of the various stages of thinking and the corresponding states of consciousness. This latter phenomenon is something of which the later developing mystical *Ishraqi* schools will make grateful use.[244]

Return to the origin (ta'wil). The principle of *ta'wil* is an opportunity to become acquainted with one of the basic principles which pervade in the Islamic world the thinking process as well as contemplation and meditation. It comes down to the idea that everything that was revealed by the highest divine being bears in itself the intention to be returned to its origin (the highest Being). Revelation means: the One communicates himself to the many, to humanity. That is the first movement.

Ta'wil indicates that what was revealed is returned to the One by humanity. This is the second movement, the one that brings the dynamic between the One and the many to completion. Philosophically it means that the highest Being will communicate himself (as light) down the several stages of Being in such a way that this communication contains in itself the potential of a return. Both from the point of view of the religious human being, as from that of the thinker—which in the large majority of cases are contained in one and the same individual, even though it is necessary to make the distinction—there is a condition attached to *ta'wil*.

In the movement of communication the initiative is with God, the highest Being. In the movement of return the initiative lies with the human being. If God takes the initiative to make himself known as and out of unicity to the many, then the initiative of the human being consists of raising himself first to a state of unicity so that he will be able to bring this dynamic to completion. If the highest Being, in an act of thinking and creating himself, makes himself known out of this act of cognition, the initiative of the human being consists of making himself known, in his turn, in thinking-being-present to himself, in other words in making himself transparent to the light.

Stages of revelation.

1. The highest Being, which rests in its own substance, is *Dhat*, Essence, pure Spirit.
2. Immediately below this begins the world of the *Jabarut*, the realm in which the revelation of Being takes place and the Pleroma of the Light Beings comes into existence.
3. This revelation of Being becomes an activity from which the creative form principles arise ceaselessly. This is the world of the creating, self-contained "images," the *Malakut*.
4. Finally, there is the world of *Molk*, also called *khalq*, the world of the created, the bodies which exist, in their state of condensation, on the border of the region of Darkness.

Thinking that is bound to the senses only generates knowledge of the world of bodies. For thinkers such as Sohrawardi such knowledge is useless if it is not developed beyond the sense world. And how does cognition rise from this *'alam-i-tabi'at* (natural world) to the higher realm of *'alam-i-malakut*? By a thinking that is able to create forms of cognition which are no longer bound to the senses. This thinking capacity is the creative power of imagination, not to be confused with the capacity of visualization which points to the sense world. It is the active capacity of imagination which is capable of dwelling in the world of images, *'alam-al-mithal*, of "sojourning" there, while it makes the essential nature of these images its own, by "holding back," "suspending itself."

Holding back means suspending the creative capacity, not allowing it to fulfill its function, adopting no form. It is about the creative capacity, not as an abstraction, but as a matter of essential being; the maintenance of the essential nature characterizes this field. This means that the human being learns through exercises to call into existence in his inner world creative images that are beings, and that these do not disintegrate into representations or precipitate into a material substratum. An example of this, which was especially practiced in some schools after Sohrawardi, was the exercise of calling into being a color, in its creative image quality, without attaching it to a physical object.

The world of active imagination. This gesture of holding back of the images (*mothol mo'allaqa*) distinguishes what was described above from the idea world of Plato (*mothol iflatuniyya*) in which the ideas precede earthly reality but cast their shadows and multiply themselves in the observable world. Neither does Sohrawardi want to equate this gesture with what for Aristotle is *hylê*, pure receptivity. The world of active imagination, the imaginative capacity, is just like the higher worlds—those of the revelation of being, the level of inspiration, and of the highest Being himself, of the intuitive level—a region of the reality of being. Only, one needs to travel the path of cognition to be able to think its increasing, rising degree of reality.

In addition to his *magnum opus*[245] Sohrawardi also left behind a number of stories which can be viewed as initiation stories. One of them, *'Aql al-Sorkh*, describes how a human being leaves the created world and makes his way in the direction of the Light Beings who form the Pleroma.[246] Out of the Pleroma a Light Being approaches him, and an encounter takes place in the in-between world, the world of creative archetypal images. The Light Being that meets the human being moves in the direction of the world of Darkness, while the human being goes in the opposite direction. As a result, the light is tempered by the effect of the polarity of Light and Darkness, and what appears as an image to the seeking human being is the color red, but in its essential nature of being. *Sorkh* means red, specifically deep magenta red[247] which arises when light has admitted the forces of darkness into itself. In this context, *'aql* means "spirit being" that has turned to the created world and therefore can be encountered in the creative image of a color.

It is not certain whether Ibn Arabi and Sohrawardi ever met. But in their spiritual legacies they found each other on one of the most wondrous paths, where thinking and experience, wisdom and practice went hand in hand: the experience of colors in their nature of image as schooling and as medium of inner connection with prophecy and revelation.

Spirituality and the Experience of Color: Nuruddin Abdurrahman Isfarayini (1242-c.1317)

Semnani (died 1336), founder of the Kubrawi order, can be considered as having been the originator of color theory as a path of esoteric schooling in Iran. He was also the most important pupil of Isfarayini. Thanks to Semnani we possess some rare data about his master, including some episodes from Isfarayini's *diarium spirituale*.

Isfarayin is a hamlet in Khorasan, in the eastern part of Iran. It is known that Isfarayini grew up in a family tradition of mysticism and Sufism. It was even said that he was born in 1242 in the *khanqah* (a term for a Sufi community or monastery) in Kasirq and was therefore also called Kasirqi. He was initiated by the Sufi master Ahmad-I-Jurpani and lived for years in a hermitage (*khalwat-e-khana*, literally: house of introspection or seclusion) in the vicinity of the *khanqah*. His fame as a pedagogue in the practice of the path of schooling, in particular of the *dhikr*,* gave him invitations from a number of circles in Baghdad. He remained and taught there for about forty years.

One of his great predecessors there was the Iranian Najm-I-Razi (died 1256),[248] who also wrote about color physiology and its path of spiritual development. It was the period of the Mongol invasions. Baghdad was destroyed in 1256, but from writings, letters and directives from Isfarayini and many others it appears that the spiritual life in monasteries and esoteric circles survived in those chaotic times.

---

* Translator's note: *Dhikr* is an Islamic devotional act, typically involving the recitation—mostly silently—of the Names of God, and of supplications taken from hadith texts and verses from the Koran, according to Sunni Islam. (Source: Wikipedia)

Isfarayini wrote a number of treatises in which he defended the proposition that in the world of *malakut*,* the spiritual leader is the center (*qutb*), but in the world of *molk* the sultan represents this center. Among other places, he wrote this in his correspondence with the Mongolian Ilkhanid ruler Oljeitu who converted to Shia in 1310. Oljeitu built a magnificent mausoleum in the north of Iran, the well-known Soltanieh, for the purpose of preserving there the remains of Imams Ali and Hussein. This monument was also a spiritual center for the Shia community.

The glory of the spirit. Isfarayini's great significance, however, lies in his pedagogical talent. He wanted to find concrete forms for the path of schooling, and formulate key concepts to give insight for spiritual thinking into the phenomena that can manifest on this path.

In a letter he wrote to Semnani we read the following:

In the region of pure presence, situated above past and future, when the Spirit (*ruh*) was sent by the Creator God to the plains of existence, He [the Spirit] left the work place of the Mysterium (*ghayb*) and manifested himself with a twofold countenance. One countenance was turned to the Divine Command of Creation (*amr*), the other was turned to the world of the created (*khalq*).

In the countenance that is turned to the world in which *amr* resounds, purity and transparency are perfect; in the countenance turned to the created world turbid darkness began to infiltrate, as a drop of water (*qutara*) is absorbed into a piece of sugar (*qand*). The countenance turned to the Command of Creation received the outpouring of the glory of the light beings and it passed this glory on to the other countenance which is turned to the world of the created.

But to carry this out another transparent substance was needed, a substance more condensed than the Spirit (*ruh*) but not yet so dense as the soul (*nafs*). This was needed so that the forming activity of the light beings, when they enter the body in order to form it, would not pulverize it. (The physical body receives its form (*tarbiyyat*) from the world of the working light beings after the will of the command of creation.) For in all its density the body does not have sufficient strength to stay together if it would directly receive the working of the glory. It would disintegrate (*tadakduk*). For this reason, the creative will has inserted the heart (*qalb, del*) between

---

* Translator's note: For *malakut* and *molk* see page 132.

the one countenance and the other, like an in-between area and link. The heart is also turned in two directions in the same way as the pen (*kalam*, which also means *Logos*, Word) is turned to the word of the creative command and to the tablet on which this command is written down. Just as the moon receives its light from the sun, in the same way the moon side of the heart receives its light from the Spirit (*ruh*). Then it transmits this light from the region of Spirit (*asman-e-ruhaniyyat*) to the region of earthly bodies and human existence (*zamin-i-qalab-i bashariyyat*).

But between the heart and the body there was need for another link (*wasita*), more condensed than the heart but not as dense and more transparent than the body. This was to prevent the outbursts of the body from damping down the subtle substance (*latifa*) of the heart and thus impeding the intentions of the Spirit (*mizaj-i-ruh*). And thus the creative will (*amr*) of the Creator fashioned between the heart and the body the in-between area of the soul (*nafs*). The soul also has two sides: one side is turned to the light that radiates to it from the heart; this is the capacity of cognition of the soul. The other side of the soul is turned to the dense darkness of the body; this is the vital soul. Between the spirit-oriented side of the soul and the heart, and between the light-oriented countenance of the heart and the command of creation, evolves the destiny of human beings and into them descended the countenance of the Spirit.[249]

Twofold dynamic. Once more we see a double dynamic (see also Avicenna): the dynamic from the regions of spirit to the world of bodies, a *condensing* dynamic, and the rising dynamic of the condensed world to an ever *increasing transparency* for the working of the light beings and the divine spirit.

It was Isfarayini's merit that he developed out of an insight into these two dynamics a doctrine of "subtle organs" (*latifah*). Obviously this was not his "discovery"! We only need to open Ibn Arabi's writings to ascertain this. But he did develop it into a teaching from which a concrete practice of schooling became possible. These subtle organs and their "placement" in the whole of a spiritual anthropology led Semnani to his color theory. The pupil clearly surpassed his master, but that is the merit of the master. What significance could a master have if he had no pupils to surpass him?

Ibn Arabi already gave profound expositions on the subtle organs, how these may be developed on the path of schooling, and their relationship to the figure of a prophet who acts as a signature for this particular organ.[250]

THE PHILOSOPHY OF FREEDOM IN IRANIAN ISLAM

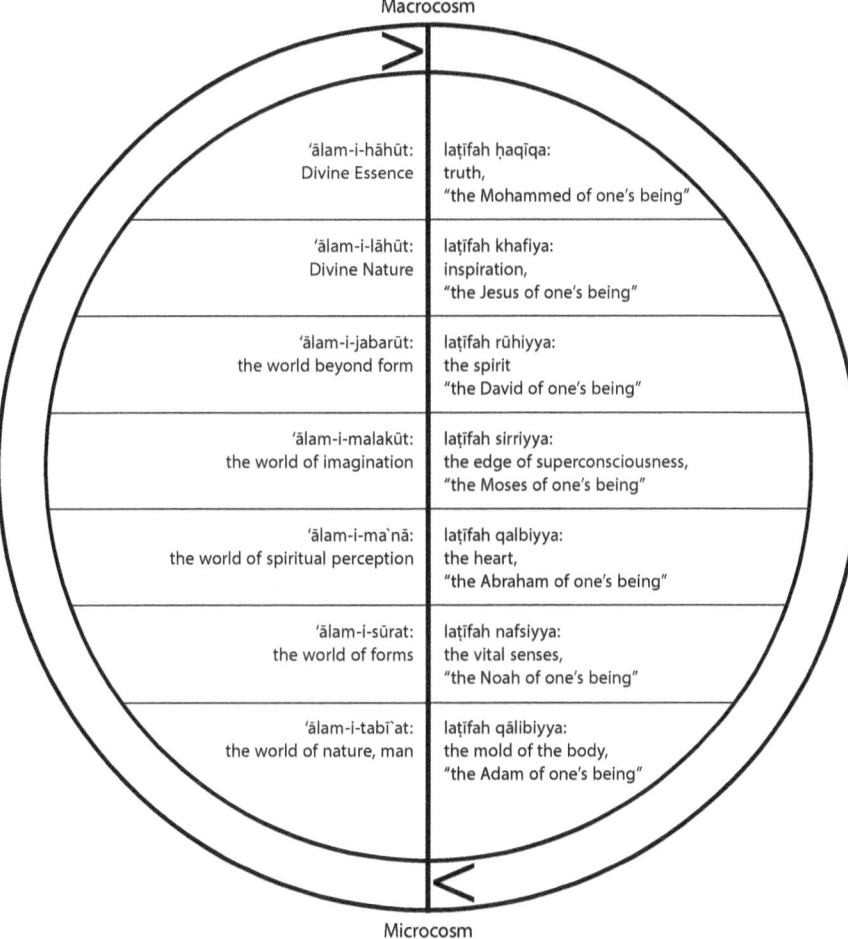

Diagram adapted from The Sense of Unity: The Sufi Tradition in Persian Architecture *by Nader Ardalan and Laleh Bakhtiar (Chicago: University of Chicago Press, 1973).*

1. *Latifah qalibiyya*: center of the subtle form of the body (Adam)
2. *Latifah nafsiyya*: center of the vital soul (Noah)
3. *Latifah qalbiyya*: center of the spiritual heart (Abraham)
4. *Latifah sirriyya*: center of the spiritual (as yet) concealed as mystery (Moses)
5. *Latifah ruhiyya*: center of the revealed light glory of the spirit (David)
6. *Latifah khafiyya*: center of the revealed life of the spirit (Jesus)
7. *Latifah haqiqat*: center of the revealed essential reality of the spirit (Mohammed).[251]

Sevenfold spectrum. A remarkable characteristic for the further development of thinking in the context of esoteric Shiism is that the stages of the exercises that lead to self-knowledge and realization of the spirit are described in concepts derived from the world and the working of the colors. All elements, from the doctrine of emanation of Avicenna and the twofold dynamic to the enlightenment of the thinking in the soul by the Spirit, find a new channel here.

In the footsteps of Sohrawardi and the schools of the *Ishraqiyyun*, human beings are described among others by Molla Sadra (1572-1640) as the beings placed between light and darkness. The changes that take place in them liberate spiritual organs that lead to perception and insight into spiritual regions.

For this reason a given color represents a real experience which occurs along the path of training and it indicates very precisely in which region pupils find themselves then, and from which specific organ of cognition they arrive at their spiritual experience. Every stage of the exercises carries the name of a prophet, and the opening of the corresponding organ of cognition is indicated by a particular color.[252]

The seven prophets in you.[253]

1. THE ADAM IN YOU

This expression points to that body which, like a delicately formed mold, forms the vessel for the "new Adam" which is to be developed in the future. The corresponding color is grey or, more precisely said, turbid light. In this stage, consciousness is still subdued although the very first germ of a new spirit body is already there.

2. THE NOAH IN YOU

Noah is the one who is able to bring all animals into one single Ark. Here we have to do with the capacity of bringing together the most diverse passions and desires of the animal soul and subjecting them to one single principle. One could also say: we mount a struggle against all these diverging tendencies, exactly like Noah had to wage a battle against his own people. The color of deep indigo blue appears here, the color of grief and separation, because every human being in his natural condition is clearly and most strongly attached to this part of the soul.

3. THE ABRAHAM IN YOU

Abraham stands in the sign of witnessing the fulfillment of a vow. Here we have to do with the moment of the promise of a numerous progeny. A first beginning is made, a first seed is planted, like the first notch in an oyster shell, from which a pearl can grow—the birth of the higher "I" that is achieved on the sixth level. The color is red. Abraham represents the heart, the seat of witnessing love.

4. THE MOSES IN YOU

Here we come to a threshold, just as Moses found himself at a threshold when God spoke to him on Mount Sinai, even though he could not see God. He is made into a friend of God (*dust-e choda*); he is brought into intimate conversation with the divine kernel, which lies in himself. The act of beholding that leads a person out of himself is now transformed into an inward beholding. The corresponding color is white, transparent and veiling at the same time. The divine continues to be concealed, but it shines through the veil, the veil which in the human soul forms a screen between the soul itself and the divine that dwells in it.

5. THE DAVID IN YOU

David is the royal man, the sovereign ruler over and within our own soul region. He represents the spiritual in the human being like a caliph, a placeholder of God, whose wisdom lies in his ability to bring to bear the divine as guiding principle over against the self-seeking strivings of the soul. Thanks to him beauty, order and harmony can reign. The color of this spiritual leadership is radiant yellow.

6. THE JESUS IN YOU

Here we enter into the most Holy of Holies into which none of the workings of the sense world or of the tendencies of the soul that is still attached to this world can penetrate. Isa (Jesus) is the prophet who is able to call every creature by its own name, with the result that they are awakened as to a new birth. The purity of Isa's heart creates the possibility to receive these names as an inspiration from the Holy Spirit. The corresponding color is radiant black, the point where one sees the inner light of the essence of everything that is rise like a sun at midnight.

7. THE MOHAMMED IN YOU

Just as Mohammed became the concluding seal on the cycle of prophets, the pupil arrives there where he is capable of becoming the seal of his own Self, putting the seal on his own higher being. The kernel that was planted in the bosom of Abraham, after the first Adam had formed the substance for a vessel which was then brought together by Noah, is now fully called to life. Moses brought this kernel to the threshold. David guided the substance into the spirit realm as a bride and sang her praises. Isa made her receptive to the highest inspiration by immersing the light of her being into the deepest reality. The color that corresponds with the stage of Mohammed is radiant green, the green which is born with jubilation out of the depth and darkness of loneliness and death.

This last and most perfect stage is called the "emerald vision." It is the color which in Iran is reflected by the sunlight from countless domes on mosques, where it changes at sunset into the softest and most subtle complementary color, the entirely immaterial magenta, a color that has not yet found a material carrier on earth and, for the present, is only able to show itself in the interplay of darkness and light.

Molla Sadra: The Highest Being is a Deed[254]

Molla Sadra lived at the time of Shah Abbas (1571-1629), who brought the Safavid Dynasty to power and proclaimed Shiism as the state religion of the Iranian Empire, which it has remained to the present day. Under this dynasty (1501-1722), which had its origin in a Sufi order founded by sheikh Safi in the fourteenth century, Iran flourished to unprecedented heights for more than two centuries, economically, politically, intellectually and culturally. We have Shah Abbas to thank for the enlargement of Isfahan which, with its magnificent blue mosques, its gardens, its beautiful bridges over the river Zayand-e Rud and its breathtaking great square, may be counted among the most beautiful cities in the world. Intensive exchanges took place in a sphere of mutual tolerance between Shah Abbas and the Mogul king Akbar the Great (1542-1605), which led to the translation into Persian of the great scriptures of Indian wisdom, including the Bhagavad Gita and the Upanishads. In this context Molla Sadra, who was born in Shiraz, became a student of Mir Damad in Isfahan, one of the leaders of the school of Sohrawardi's *Ishraqiyyun*. It was only one of the many schools that would flourish in Isfahan, Shiraz and other places. Within these schools a movement developed to give Sufism, which was traditionally more connected with Sunna, also a place in Shiism.

Molla Sadra's premise. For Molla Sadra, just as for his great predecessors, thinking begins in the dynamic unity of Being, the *wahdat al-wujud*, which is grounded in the divine essence. This dynamic unity is not a result, but an ongoing process of God's self-realization. The central question is then how we can conceive of a connection between this highest Being and the multiplicity of beings that owe their existence to the one Being.

Avicenna is Molla Sadra's greatest source of inspiration, together with Sohrawardi and Ibn Arabi. Most of all, however, he is a thinker in the context of Shiism and the teaching of the Twelve Imams. His thinking will therefore move in the framework of two cycles. The first cycle is the series of prophets which is sealed by Mohammed (see *The seven prophets in you* on page 138). This cycle is characterized by revelation. Shiism proclaims that this cycle is followed by a second one, the cycle of the Imams or the *nalaat*. This cycle is characterized by inwardness. The two cycles—the one outwardly oriented (exoteric), the other inwardly oriented (esoteric)—belong together like the two sides of a coin. In contrast to the cycle of the prophets (*nobowwat*), the cycle of the *nalaat* has not yet come to an end. For the twelfth Imam, who has withdrawn from the world of manifestation, will return at the end of time. Only then will the full cycle of the development of earth and humanity be fulfilled.

If we can view prophecy as an event in which what is hidden in God is revealed to the outside world by the word of the prophets, then the reverse takes place in the cycle of the *awliyya*. That which was revealed by the prophets is now turned inward; it is absorbed by the spiritual organs of cognition of human beings and made their own. In this way these organs of cognition are awakened in their activity. This is an open process which, while it has a beginning (the first Imam), will not reach its completion until the return of the twelfth Imam. In other words, we are on the way to a future that is still open.

Mohammed, in his own person, closed the long series of revelations that were given to humanity in the course of time. He did not bring new revelation, but an extract, a concentrated summary of all revelations, a kind of archetypal revelation which pulls the cycle of revelations together in itself like a seed. And this seed now begins to sprout.

The cycle of the *awliyya* represents a growth process that emerges from this germ. The process is not complete. The secret leap from seed to germ can be viewed as an area where the transformation from openness to inwardness, from exoteric to esoteric, takes place.

In his great work *The Four Journeys* (*al-Asfar al-arba'in*) Molla Sadra describes this alternation between outer and inner as journeys that always take place between different points of departure and destinations. Obviously, we have to do here with journeys in the "imaginal world," spiritual journeys.[255]

The first journey departs from creation with the ultimate destination of "One who, alone, is genuine and true," *al-Haqq*. At this stage, the traveler acquires insight into the nature of the created, how form and matter interpenetrate, how a being is composed out of essence and accident.*

The second journey begins in Truth (*al-Haqq*) and leads to Truth through Truth. During this stage, the pilgrim fathoms the divine being and the divine names, and dwells in the transcendent world of God's reality.

In the third journey the traveler returns to existence as a creature, but the point of departure is the divine reality: "with God through God." This stage gives insight into the ranks of the hierarchies of the Intelligences, in other words, the ranks of beings who descend from the highest level down to the created world.

Finally, the fourth journey leads through the created world in which the pilgrim now travels with God in creation (*bi-l-Haqq fi-l-Khalq*). But the world of creation is now seen from the inside and is a witness, in the multiplicity of its forms of appearance, of the original unity (*tawhid*) of God to which everything returns.

Parallel to these contemplations on the possible connections between necessary Being (which is its own cause) and being which is not its own cause, in which Avicenna's radical distinction can be found again as the central theme, Molla Sadra also developed an epistemology. Here also we see a continuation of Avicenna's epistemology, in which cognition was defined as the actualization of the capacity of cognition by the work of the Intellectus Agens, the Angel of Revelation. That is not a process that proceeds automatically. Avicenna strongly emphasized that the extent to which actualization is able to take place depends on the capacity to receive—a capacity that can only be prepared by and in the soul, and is therefore necessarily different for each human being. At this point, Sohrawardi spoke of cognition in and through presence which leads to self-knowledge.

Here Molla Sadra's epistemology goes a step farther. Cognitive capacity and that which is cognized become one. This is not the same thing as fusing one with the other. The fact that they can become one is grounded in the identity of cognition and being. Following Avicenna and Sohrawardi, Molla Sadra described

---

* Translator's note: *Accident*, as used in philosophy, indicates an attribute which may or may not belong to a subject, without affecting its essence.

how the cognitive capacity is awakened (actualized) in the soul by the Angel of Revelation (Intellectus Agens) and that this cognition always also encompasses self-knowledge. Self-knowledge means becoming present to oneself. Self-knowledge leads to self-realization, to a higher form of existence. It is the kind of thinking which ultimately leads to becoming, to development. This development leads away from multiplicity, from the particular, to an ever more intense union with self. The germ of individual freedom lies here.

Freedom arises in a process of self-knowledge and self-realization. Of course, this is not the same thing as a process of self-liberation that leads to arbitrariness. Self-realization fundamentally differs from self-involvement. On this path, which leads from cognition to self-realization, human beings practice in the first place what was bestowed on them as their birth right in creation. They possess the capacity of becoming transparent to themselves and, in this process, all of creation also becomes transparent to them. This building up of insight into oneself and into everything else is none other than realizing, through thinking in the spirit, the unity of God which is the ground of all things.

Thinking—traveling back and forth between the manifested and the hidden—only becomes thinking in the sign of the spirit when "travelers take care that their inner schooling is nourished by philosophical contemplation and, on the other hand, their philosophizing never takes place without spiritual exercise." This is not an either-or but a both-and prerequisite. It is the reason for Molla Sadra's severe judgment of some Sufis, who exhibited a certain disdain for the practice of philosophy. And in the prologue to his *Four Journeys* he also lashed out at the representatives of the philosophy of law who considered themselves too exalted for spiritual practice.

A radical ontology. The radical nature of Molla Sadra's ontology (being is a deed!) can easily escape notice for a modern reader, because the verb "to be" in ordinary use of language also serves as a linking verb between a noun and a predicate. It links an attribute to a subject. Henry Corbin, who was a pupil of Martin Heidegger, speaks in this respect of a "devaluation" of the verb "to be." It is possible to use beside the verb "to be" the verb "to exist," but this does not avoid the danger of a change in meaning. Besides, it shows a lack of precision when these two words are used as equivalents. "God is" and "God exists" are not interchangeable statements.

There is more at stake than just a nuance. The English "exist" is derived from the Latin *exsistere*, a composite word pointing to that out of which (*ex* = out; *sistere* = to place) one exists, to the origin of existence. Thus Descartes justifiably formulated his famous conclusion *ergo sum* (therefore I am) using the verb *esse* (to be) and not *exsistere*. What counted for him was to deduce his existence as being from the origin of his own thinking, and not from a being outside himself.

In this regard, Arabic and Persian possess a greater linguistic palette. In Arabic the root of the verb "to be" is w-j-d and literally means "to find, to meet." Being in the sense of an active deed becomes *al-wud-jud*. In the passive form it means "being found" or "having been found, having become" (*mawjud*) and is used for that which is (*ens**), that which is found or has become, and has thus been called into existence. This corresponds with the meaning of *exsistere* in Latin. Therefore, this approach does not permit the expression "God exists," for it would imply that God "was found" or "had become" and therefore had his origin outside Himself.

The Arabic verb also permits the use of an active "to cause to exist," the causative *ijad*. And this can also be turned into a passive form: "that which, as existing thing or being, was done or made." Then it expresses the condition of being in existence, in the sense of *exsistere*. In this context the verb *wjd* is never used as a linking verb.

The highest Being (*ousia* in Greek) is not that which has existence, but that which engenders being as a deed. For Molla Sadra, God is not a being that exists in the sense that it possesses existence as it would possess an attribute that is linked to its being. In God, being and attribute coincide. Causing to exist and existing as a condition cannot be distinguished from each other in God. This is the highest reality which is at the same time truth: *al-Haqqiqat*.[256]

Threefold birth. Just as in the case of Avicenna who, in contrast with the Aristotelians, transferred the principle of individualization from the body to the soul, Molla Sadra also achieves a revolutionary breakthrough in the pattern of thinking. In scholastic thinking, the essence—the sum of all one's separate characteristics as *ens*, that which signifies one's essential being—is something that precedes one's existence as *ens*. Essence comes before existence. First one is a "someone" and as such one then enters into concrete existence. Molla Sadra reverses this! First there is the active deed of coming into existence, and out of this deed, and the intensity with which it is performed, arises who one is. "The reality of all that is, is grounded in the act to be; the reality of who someone is, this is one's act to be."[257] The immediate

---

* Translator's note: *Ens* is the present participle of the Latin verb *esse*, to be.

consequence of this is that it is not predetermined who one is, but that one must first come into existence through an act, a deed, to become who one is! It is self-evident that this deed, which brings one into existence, is not the birth of the physical body. If so, this would have happened all at once! In fact, however, this deed is repeatedly performed, in the course of which its intensity can be increased. This deed is directly related to the act of cognition. It is this act—which also means that one makes oneself receptive to the influence of the Intellectus Agens (the noetic capacity)—that enables one to achieve active cognition. Cognition and self-realization coincide here.

As the intensity increases, the essence also changes (*al-wojud al-jawhari*). If the intensity weakens, the essence also weakens. Growth in intensity of the essence increases the potential of cognition. It becomes possible to arrive at cognition of a reality that no longer requires a physical bearer. The stages of cognition in relation to the ranks of reality are the same as those which Sohrawardi and Ibn Arabi developed. Molla Sadra's thinking is in their footsteps, but with this decisive difference that he does not begin with the essence, but with the deed to realize oneself in existence. This means that each being is subject to change and transformation, and that there can be development which becomes more and more strongly individual. The potential for this lies in the soul, again in complete agreement with Avicenna. However, with Avicenna we find the principle that existence is derived from the essential being and not, as with Molla Sadra, that the act of being engenders the essence.

Molla Sadra recognizes the possibility that the human being is born three times during his life. That is an obvious conclusion from the reversal of existence and essence.

The first birth is the same for all human beings: it is the birth from the body of the mother through which one enters into the world of the created. Although arrived on earth, one is still lying "in the cradle" as regards the rest of reality.

The second birth occurs when the human being is born to the reality of supersensible worlds as these actualize themselves in the soul by performing the act of being, which is at the same time an act of cognition. Sadra calls this second birth the "little resurrection" (*qiyamat soghra*). But here too, one is still lying "in the cradle" as regards the great resurrection (*qiyamat kobra*). One is still in an in-between world (*barzakh*) between the first and third births.

The third birth constitutes in a certain sense an octave leap. That which had become transparent in the soul through self-knowledge is now born in the highest spiritual realms, those of the Intelligences of the Cherubim. This is the birth into the spirit.

The possibilities of growth and development are present in the in-between world. It is the soul which plays the key role to make such growth possible. If it turns to the body and the world of the manifested, it remains asleep in the first cradle. If it actively makes itself receptive to the influence of the Angel of Revelation (Intellectus Agens, often also called Holy Spirit), with the result that it achieves self-realization and self-knowledge, then the in-between period of the Little Resurrection begins. From this cradle it will be awakened by the "trumpet with the shattering beam of light" to be born into the world of the Great Resurrection.

Thinking is Presence in Spirit: Mehdi Hairi Yazdi

What is thinking? What is its purpose? What does thinking signify in the totality of human nature, and in the whole of the plan of creation? We no longer need to be surprised that this question is met in a most profound manner by a series of personalities who, independently of what has been taking place in the western world, especially since Descartes, found a path of thinking very much their own—a path on which discursive thought does not play first fiddle. A prominent modern representative of this stream is Mehdi Hairi Yazdi (1923-1999) who studied and taught philosophy in, among other places, Canada and the United States. In 1979 he returned to Iran where he taught mostly at the University of Tehran until his death.

In a work he wrote in English, Yazdi developed the theme of "knowledge by presence" (*'ilm al hudur*). In recent years, there has been a great deal of interest, also in other areas than philosophy, in "presence and presencing."[258] It has to be mentioned that this expression was not invented by Yazdi in the framework of his thinking. It is a well-known technical term in Iranian philosophy that was first used by Sohrawardi as part of a movement to systematize terminology. It is extremely difficult to render this term correctly in another language. Yazdi published a summary of the most frequently used terms that were derived from Sohrawardi's work and translated into English.[259]

Mehdi Yazdi received a classical education in philosophy, theology and *'irfan** in Qom, and later he studied at the University of Tehran, where he earned his doctorate in theology in 1952. He was also interested in western epistemology and the methods of science as such. For a number of years he thoroughly immersed himself in the works of Molla Sadra, Avicenna and Nasir al-Din

---

* Translator's note: *'Irfan* literally means knowing/awareness. The term is often translated as gnosis, however it also refers to Islamic mysticism. (Source: Wikipedia)

Tusi (1201-1274) under the supervision of the most famous teachers of his time, including Ruhallah Khomeini. During his sojourn in the West he studied with the same passionate interest the works of Kant, Hegel, Russell and Wittgenstein. Out of his deeply rooted connection with the age-old tradition of thinking in Iran, he delved into the problems that were then being discussed in western epistemology, hoping this would enable him to make a contribution to Islamic philosophy as a whole.

Mehdi Yazdi was not the only Iranian philosopher in the twentieth century who continued his training in the West, or who was open to what was developing in philosophy in the western world. One of those who had the same interest was Allamah Tabatabaei (1892-1981) from Tabriz, Iran, one of the most original and profound Islamic thinkers. As a result of his contacts with Corbin, Seyyed Hossein Nasr and William Chittick, the idea arose to develop a school for comparative gnosis. Abdolkarim Soroush is another thinker who wants to build a bridge between Islamic and western philosophy.

Yazdi, however, was unique in that he made western thinking his own in order to test it to the philosophical discourse as this has developed in the Islamic world. And, the other way around, to expose the thinking of the spirit, with which he was so familiar and which was so much part of him, to the light of the discursive thinking predominant in the West in the past few centuries.

Yazdi's great theme was "knowledge in and by presence" which implies a quite specific state of consciousness.[260]

Two paths to cognition. Yazdi distinguished two forms of knowledge: *knowledge by correspondence* and *knowledge by presence*. To establish the difference Yazdi described the thinking processes for these two forms phenomenologically. What interested him in this is the question whether there exists a form of thinking in which the classical dichotomy between subject and object is no longer operative.

Yazdi's first step in this direction was to describe what is in fact going on when someone says: "I think." The "I" that makes the statement "I think" and the "I" that thinks are not two different entities; they are one and the same. I know from immediate inner experience that this is so. There is no need for an interposition of a representation in this case, as though I would first have to make myself a representation of my own "I" in order to arrive at the statement that I think. It is important to realize that we are dealing here with a well-defined situation, namely that of thinking!

This immediate inner knowledge (intuition), in the transparency of the act of cognition itself, is what Yazdi, consistent with Sohrawardi, called "knowledge by presence." The thinking process will therefore have to be described.

Because of his intimate familiarity, acquired over many years, with the representatives of western philosophy (Descartes, Hume, Kant, Hegel, but also Heidegger, Russell, Wittgenstein, Popper, Habermas—with whom he enters into dialog in his works) Yazdi had the ability to uncover with great precision the characteristics of logical-discursive thinking in general, and the subject/object split in particular. On the other hand, as regards knowledge by presence, Yazdi could boast of being part of a centuries-old tradition within Iranian philosophy where Avicenna, Sohrawardi and Molla Sadra not only laid the foundation of thinking in the light of the spirit but, and this is by far the most important, created a language that can be used as an instrument to express the individual moments of this thinking in its nature as a process.

The triad of the thinking process. It is important that when Yazdi, in the footsteps of his predecessors, described the thinking process, he always spoke in terms of a triad: the one who cognizes, the object of cognition, and the thinking which, as an activity in process, builds the bridge between the two.

In *analytical cognition* (as opposed to discursive thinking) the object of cognition is external to the one who cognizes. Thinking must make use of representations that are already available. Truth arises when it can be demonstrated that there is agreement between this representation and the external object. This type of cognition has caused all kinds of questions as to methodological certainty. The various points of view in this (Habermas, Popper, Russell) continue to define western philosophy into our time.

In *knowledge by presence* the object of cognition does not appear in a different realm than that of the one who cognizes. In other words, that to which the activity of thinking is directed, appears within the same field as that of the one who performs the thinking activity. This process points to self-knowledge; however, it must not be confused with introspection in which the self is treated as an external element before the gaze of the cognizer, and in which representations of the self need to be made. Nor does the thinker become both subject *and* object. It is no *unio mystica*! Yazdi described mystical experience and its translation—again we see the great importance of language and its use—as a particular form of knowledge by presence.

But in this second type of cognition the ground pattern of the triad remains the pre-eminent characteristic. It is the dynamic between the three elements which makes cognition into knowledge by presence. The role of thinking, and making this transparent, remains a necessary condition. Not self-analysis, nor fusion, but a totally awake presence in the act of thinking itself—it amounts to being present in oneself. It is a thinking that can carry itself through the process of the activity of thinking.

Yazdi considers all other forms of cognition, meaning cognition in which the object is an external factor, as derived from this self-carrying thinking. And while in thinking by consensus there always remains a factor of uncertainty, which had to be overcome by Cartesian doubt, Yazdi considered knowledge by presence as "living in the immediacy of truth." Between the cognizer and the object of cognition there is no representation that has to function as a bridge between subject and object. Both cognizer and the object of cognition are of identical "nature." In the dynamic of the process of cognition this is mutually recognized, and it becomes an experience of "wholeness" that may be compared with an experience of happiness.

Liberation. For discursive thinking the subject/object split is a condition. It is this duality between cognizer and the object of cognition which constitutes this thinking. Knowledge so gained is knowledge by consensus, correspondence. That which I know (the subjective pole of the thinking process) and the known (the objective pole) must be in agreement with each other for thinking to provide certainty and lead to truth.

Knowledge by presence takes place outside of this duality. It is beyond the subject/object split. Yazdi described this as a liberation from the constraint of having to produce proof, because this form of cognition needs no proof in the nature of consensus. Proof is needed when the object of cognition is made external. Then there is a need for a representation to, one could say, internalize the object of cognition. And the principle of consensus then reigns as the criterion of truth or untruth. But this same principle cannot be applicable in the case of knowledge by presence.

Yazdi did not reject the truth criterion of consensus. He demonstrated that this can only be applicable in the case of logical-discursive thinking and knowledge by consensus on the basis of the subject/object split. However, when it is a case of knowledge by presence, a different criterion is needed. This criterion is inherent in the activity of the act of thinking itself. The activity of thinking creates a unitary field in which the cognizer and the cognized appear as part of one and the same field. The object of cognition is in this case immanent and needs no representation. Because of this it is liberated from the need to show consensus. This does not mean that the cognizer and the cognized coincide. Yazdi spoke here of correlation within the same field of existence.

The "I" is not a thing. For Yazdi a clear example of knowledge by presence is the self-knowledge that arises during this process. This is not (yet) the self-knowledge that can be developed in the course of an ever-increasing intensity of the capacity of cognition, but is a kind of prelude to it. Neither is it self-knowledge through psychology, which works with representation regarding oneself. It is self-knowledge in the sense of becoming inwardly completely transparent to oneself as a reality. In other words: not *knowledge regarding oneself*, but *becoming present in and to oneself*. No *represented* "I," which continues to be a "thing," but an "I" that becomes manifest in *presence*.

In the simplest case, for instance when I make the statement "I know that my neighbor is at home," there is a knowing (the object of knowing) which I connect in a self-evident way with the "I" who knows this (the knower). Also when I leave out the "I know" and say only "My neighbor is at home," I still relate the knowing to the one who knows, namely I myself. There could not be any knowing if it cannot at the same time be related to someone who knows.

When we consider a statement such as "I know myself," it is even more evident that I connect "myself," as the object of knowing, with the "I" who is the knower.

The underlying motive for Yazdi's argument was an implicit disagreement with Russell and his analytical school. The reality of the "I," whether it appears on the side of the knower or of the object of knowing, can only be known through knowledge by presence. If it would also be possible to know it as representation (knowledge by correspondence), then it is reduced to an "it." But then it loses all reality. Then it is a word that can be used at will in the game of language. But in the case of the "I" this nominalistic language game does not work, said Yazdi: "The language game of 'I' therefore is radically different from anything else expressed by it." The "I" which was meant by Yazdi, in the line of his great predecessors, is the "I" which reveals itself in its full reality in and through the act of cognition. The reality of my "I" is experienced immediately—i.e., without anything intermediate!—in the activity of my thinking process. It is noteworthy that he applied the logical argumentation of Sohrawardi to demonstrate this.

There are some one thousand years between Sohrawardi and Bertrand Russell, but that does not mean that a confrontation between their two different paths to knowledge could not be of great current interest. Among all possible objects, there is at least one, and only one, which does not derive its existence from another object, and that is the "I." The "I" comes into being and exists in the self-contemplation that takes place in the act of cognition. "This sort of 'I' can never be converted under any circumstance unto an 'it.'"[261]

Yazdi spoke of an "I" that has become one and is singular, and in which all split has been overcome. Even more, this "I" is at the same time the *locus manifestationis* (place of manifestation) of a human being's essence, and this essence itself. Thinkers such as Avicenna and Molla Sadra would have recognized this in the *Ayat an-Nur*, the Light Verse from the Koran (Sura 24:35; see below) in which the expression is used *nur 'ala nur*, "light over light."

For Yazdi this was "presence."

The Freedom Impulse in Context

Freedom is the greatest good of every human being, the highest possible achievement and therefore the highest to be striven for.[262] But freedom is no abstract concept! This means that freedom always appears in a context. The context differs not only depending on the age and the culture, but also depending on the person in question. The fact that the freedom impulse manifests differently in different contexts does not obviate the essence of freedom. Indeed, it is inherent in the idea of freedom that it will manifest differently in different situations.

For freedom is present as a natural tendency, an inner potential. In this regard no one is excluded from the possibility of freedom. But the natural tendency asks to be realized. Whether it can be transformed into reality depends both on inner and outer circumstances. This explains the fact that in different ages or cultures freedom makes use of different ways of expressing itself. It is not the natural tendency toward freedom which causes such differences. As potential, freedom is one and the same for everyone. However, the manner in which people seek to realize this freedom within the given context of their time and culture causes differences—indeed, even contradictions.

In large parts of the world today people have the opinion that freedom, as the foundation for the rights of the individual, presupposes that the public domain must be free of any expression of religious persuasion. Religion is strictly a private affair and cannot as such have a role in public life. Church and State must in principle be separate from each other. This separation, an attainment of the Age of Enlightenment, is the test for the degree of progress of a society. Viewed from western secularized society, every form of government in which this separation has not been accomplished is, by definition, behind in its development compared with what in the industrialized world is considered to be the only correct way of realizing freedom. It is an open question whether this is indeed the only possible manner in which the natural tendency toward freedom can be transformed into reality.

Abdolkarim Soroush is one of those who see other possibilities.[263] First and foremost he points to the difficulty for western discourse to place rights and duties within the same horizon. It often seems that in a western democracy all kinds of rights can be demanded, but that these rights are not, as a matter of course, brought into connection with the duties that are an immediate part of them. Freedom of speech, for instance, is a right, but it also entails duty in the sense of a responsibility for the relationships within which this right is exercised. On the other hand, fulfilling a duty also generates rights. In such a view the individual is always an individual-in-relationship, with the result that rights and duties are in a kind of mutual interaction. Freedom comes into being in this interaction, in the possibility to weigh rights and duties in regard to each other and bring them into balance.

Naturally, circumstances will always exist that will curtail this striving for freedom. There may be inner circumstances which cause a person to renounce this exercise of balance for one reason or another, and to fulfill a prescribed duty. But there may just as well be outer circumstances in which a strict interpretation of the rules of life make an autonomous, personal weighing of duty against right impossible.

Also in western secularized societies there are similarly ways to restrict the possibility to realize the natural tendency toward freedom. The unfettered exercise of a right of self-realization that takes no account of any relationships is just as much a restriction as the universal pressure to consume, which is viewed as a "privilege."

These very different paths to the realization of the natural tendency toward freedom have a history which, both for the Islamic and the Christian world, are manifested most clearly in the way they have developed the role of thinking in relation to the freedom impulse.

Freedom impulse and the image of the human being. The possibility to think the concept of freedom is conditioned by a particular view of the human being, namely as a multi-layered being. In current western thinking the idea of a one-dimensional human being is predominant; see Herbert Marcuse's book with this title.[264]

In Islamic thinking, in Iranian philosophy in particular, the human being is still viewed as possessing body, soul and spirit. The image of the human being as a triad is the foundation on which the many branches of philosophy stand, whether epistemology, logic, theology, metaphysics or philosophy of science. Contrary to the famous maxim and first sentence of a treatise by Rousseau: "Humans are born free and they are everywhere in chains,"[265] the point of departure here is that human beings are born as limited and externally determined beings, but are capable of developing to freedom. In order to realize this a multi-layering of their nature is necessary. If human nature would be one-dimensional, limited to the physical, change would be possible but not development. Development presumes a transformation of the given. As Avicenna had already indicated, this possibility lies in the soul, in the extent to which it opens itself to the wake-up call of the spiritual principle which leads to self-knowledge and self-realization. Or, as Molla Sadra calls it when he speaks of the threefold birth, the key moment is the Little Resurrection that takes place in the soul as preparation for the Great Resurrection in the Spirit. In a thinker of our time such as Yazdi we find this, among others, in the threefold dynamic of every process of cognition.

Epilogue: Polishing the Mirror—The Soul (Al-Ghazali and Avicenna)

For Al-Ghazali, philosophy was not capable of answering clearly and conclusively the most important questions it was being asked, and he deeply distrusted its practitioners, in particular Avicenna.[266] This did not prevent him from making grateful use of Avicenna's mystical commentaries on the *Ayat al-Nur* (the "light verses" of the Koran, Sura 24:35), and their philosophical implications, his treatise *Mishkat al-Anwar*, in which he describes a systematic approach to the mystical way using light-metaphysics.[267]

Although these two men are known in history as each other's opponents—maybe not quite justifiably so—they did share one area where they approached each other, namely that of the mystical way that is a continuation of both theology and philosophy, and where both areas converge.

A theme they both wrote about, each from his own point of view, is the well-known and much loved theme of the soul as mirror, and its polishing. It seems as if in the world of Islam philosophy and its continuation, mysticism, have exhibited a special partiality for this image of the soul as mirror. The mirror receives and reflects that which it, itself, is not. To make this possible a twofold action is required: the soul must purify itself from that which impedes the mirroring while, in addition, it must polish itself so that it becomes ever better able to "render back" what it receives. The soul thus surrenders to a higher principle and then reflects this higher principle. In connection with this purification, Ghazali speaks of the rust spots that tarnish the reflecting surface. That refers to the soul to the extent that it surrenders to the world of the senses which, in its turn, is again a "reflection."

The point is not a Gnostic rejection of the manifested, sense-perceptible world as such. The manifested world is the Book of Creation and carries the signature of its Creator. Consequently, this world is intrinsically good. Ghazali's point is that one should not fall into the error of confusing the manifested world, which is a reflection, with that which is the origin of this reflection. One should not confuse the mirror with the reality that is mirrored in it! The soul is given this task in the manner of a *jihad*, a great inner struggle. Just as rust is a corruption of the surface of the mirror, the soul must resist corruption of itself. When we want to develop the soul as mirror, so that truth can be reflected in it, we face two tasks: purification and polishing.

"The moment that the highest truth can reflect itself in the soul, the possibility arises in the soul to share in this truth. To a certain extent the soul can identify itself with this truth, and yet it remains a separate entity."[268] The act of polishing the soul is for Ghazali the *dhikr*, the ceaseless remembrance of the reality of the divine. It is noteworthy that Ghazali characterizes the angelic hierarchies as those beings in whom the mirror reflects in complete harmony with the mirroring surface. Neither purification nor polishing are necessary. Only in the human being is the surface of the mirror corrupted and must first be purified and polished so it can perform its function.

For Avicenna the first and foremost point of importance is that the soul has to manifest an intention, a direction indicating its will to perfect itself. In order to perfect itself, the soul has to move from a condition of pure potential to the realization of this potential. This intention transforms the soul into a "niche" (*mishkat*), within which the light can be kindled. The soul now prepares itself, in the manner of a reflecting surface, to receive the light. This readiness of the soul to receive that which it, itself, is not, is like the consecrated oil of the olive tree "whose oil is well-nigh luminous" (Sura 24:35 below).

Finally, in its readiness to receive, intuitive capacities of cognition are awakened in the soul. This is "Light upon Light" (ibid.). Ultimately, what takes place in direct cognition is actualized—it becomes reality. It is the human capacity of cognition which becomes active. And it is lighted by the Intellectus Agens, the cognitive capacity that begins to work in the soul.²⁶⁹

Both Ghazali and Avicenna agree that it is the task of the human being to prepare himself in order that the soul, as mirror, may share in the spirit: *nur ala nur*, light upon light.

> Allah is the Light of the heavens and the earth. The Parable of His Light is as if there were a Niche and within it a Lamp: the Lamp enclosed in Glass: the glass as it were a brilliant star: Lit from a blessed Tree, an Olive, neither of the east nor of the west, whose oil is well-nigh luminous, though fire scarce touched it: Light upon Light! Allah doth guide whom He will to His Light: Allah doth set forth Parables for men: and Allah doth know all things. (Sura 24:35)

Part 4

Rudolf Steiner on Islam
John van Schaik

Methodology, Part 1

The work Rudolf Steiner (1861-1925) left behind is voluminous. He wrote 28 books and gave over 6000 lectures in Europe, most of which have been collected in about 330 volumes. There has hardly been any critical scientific commentary on this material. This is really needed because Rudolf Steiner's spiritual legacy is not without its problems. Some of these are mentioned here:

> 1. In general, the subjects of the lectures were chosen because someone had asked Steiner a specific question. For instance, one of his last lecture cycles in 1924 took place because agrarians in the vicinity of Breslau (now Wroclaw in Poland) asked him for it. As a result, the indications Rudolf Steiner gave for biodynamic agriculture seem to be attuned to the agricultural situation in the area of Breslau. Another example is that many lectures before World War I were given for members of the Esoteric School in an (irregular) Free Mason context. Steiner's lecture cycles therefore have to be read in a specific context. This may mean that Steiner dealt with one and the same subject in different ways for different audiences. Thus, when reading such lectures, it is important to keep the specific context in mind.

> 2. In the lecture cycles it is not always clear at which moments Rudolf Steiner was inspired and spoke out of "supersensible insight." Often this was not the

case, and then he presented general knowledge of his own time without mentioning his sources (which is normal in lectures unless one uses a direct quote). So far there has been little critical research as to the sources of his views. Clearly, in his statements on Islam he demonstrably presented more than once the general knowledge of his time (see part 1).

3. In addition, the stenographers who recorded his lectures sometimes made mistakes. Fortunately, this has received attention in the recent editions of the *Gesamtausgabe* (Complete Works, or CW).

4. Then there is the problem of "advancing insight," the fact that Steiner presented a particular subject differently, for instance, in 1906 than he did in 1924. That is notably the case with his Christology. In 1906, Steiner—cautiously—began to develop his Christology. But it was then still embedded in his theosophical way of speaking. Gradually Steiner emancipated himself from this and his Christology developed a western anthroposophical character. We need to take such developments into account.

5. Steiner dealt with many subjects from different angles. The reason is that truth has different sides, he said. The inevitable consequence is that the reader regularly has to shift his thinking. Sometimes it even seems as if Steiner was contradicting himself. That is trying, but it does foster mobility in thinking.

6. In regard to Steiner's statements on Islam there are a few specific problems. Steiner did not devote a lecture cycle to Islam; there is not even one whole lecture on Islam. His statements on Islam are spread over his entire work, often as illustrations of the subject he was speaking about. It is therefore a risky exercise to pull these statements out of their context. For instance, Steiner spoke of the fatalistic character of the "Father religion" of Islam. That sounds serious, unless you take into account that a few pages later he said the same thing of the Christianity of his time.

7. Anthroposophy, in its essence, is a form of "esoteric Christianity." From that angle, Steiner sharply criticized the Church and the traditional Christianity of his time. But from the same esoteric point of view he also viewed "common" traditional Islam. That produces a "dishonest" comparison: Steiner should have compared his esoteric Christianity with esoteric Islam, namely Sufism. But he did not do that. Strangely enough, Steiner never said anything at all about

Sufism. That is even more conspicuous because his great example Goethe was an ardent admirer of the Islamic mystic Hafez (1320-1431).

Methodology, Part 2

When studying Rudolf Steiner's scattered statements on Islam, we therefore have to take into account the methodological remarks made above. But how can we do that? I am using for this the tried and trusted method of so-called "threefold exegesis" as it was used in the Middle Ages and continues to be used for text analysis. My version of this is as follows:

> 1. I take a specific theme and compare, for instance, all of Steiner's statements on the theme relating to Islam—such as Islam as a "Father religion"—confronting them with each other in the process. I do not make an historical analysis of the texts; I do not consider a possible development in Steiner's thinking about Islam (which would actually be needed).

> 2. I then trace, to the extent possible, whether Steiner's statements are unique or whether they are in agreement with general views held in his time. I include references to earlier chapters in this book.

> 3. The result is that I have collected a number of statements that are evidently unique and in which Steiner shows authentic insight. If you will you may call this "supersensible insight."

Thus, with this method, I have filtered Steiner's unique statements on Islam out of the totality of his statements. These unique statements are relevant to the questions we are struggling with today. The remainder of Steiner's statements are time bound and dated, even though we continue to hear such dated statements even in our time.

Procedure

In this chapter I am focused on three themes:

1. Islam is a "Father religion";
2. The "impulse of Gondishapur", Sorat and Islam; and
3. Jesus (Isa) in Islam.

These subjects do not cover all Steiner's statements on Islam; that would require a separate book. But these themes are the most relevant ones in relation to our subject of the freedom impulse of Islam.

For each theme I first recapitulate a number of statements that seem to be of dominant importance. These are in most cases the same statements that are dominant among anthroposophists. Then I investigate whether there are statements that mitigate this dominant picture. This leads to conclusions.

I do not literally quote Steiner's statements but paraphrase them to some extent. The endnotes contain explanatory remarks on Steiner's text.*

Islam is a "Father Religion"

Explanation

Islam is a "Father religion" while Christianity is a "Son religion." A Father God religion leads to unfreedom while the idea of the Son of God leads to freedom.

The Dominant Picture: Predestination

Quotations from the work of Rudolf Steiner:

> Mohammedanism[270] is based on one divine being that is the ground of all that is (CW 51, *Über Philosophie, Geschichte und Literatur*, November 8, 1904).

> It is a religion that takes no account of the Christ impulse,[271] but it is a revival in a different form of the old unitary god of Moses. It is the monotheistic, unitary god of Jahve (or Jehova) under the symbol of the moon (CW 124, *Background to the Gospel of St. Mark*, March 13, 1911; CW 235, *Karmic Relationships*, Vol. I, March 16, 1924).

> Allah is omnipotent so that everything is predestined (*Vorherbestimmung*). Everything, every human deed, is written in the book of Allah. That is the doctrine of *kismet*[272] which, for the Turks, leads to a fatalistic view of life (CW 167, *Gegenwärtiges und Vergangenes im Menschengeiste*, May 23, 1916).

---

* Translator's note: The paraphrased passages were translated unchanged from Dutch into English.

A moon religion is a distinct Father religion, as was the Hebrew-Jewish religion which Mohammed brings in a new form. The forces proceeding from the Father are forces that created the physical in the whole of creation. The Father God is the ruler of everything which tends to fatalism in the human being, because one is born with it and because it works like nature forces. The Trinity—in which the Son brings freedom—is rejected by Mohammed (CW 240, *Karmic Relationships*, Vol. VI, April 16, 1924).

The world is a monotheistic expression of God (CW 272, *Geisteswissenschaftliche Erläuterungen zu Goethes "Faust,"* Vol I, April 11, 1915).

Allah, Eloha, is an ahrimanic imitation or pale reflection of the Elohim, but comprehended monotheistically (CW 300a, *Conferences with Teachers of the Waldorf School in Stuttgart, 1919-1924*, Vol. I, June 9, 1920).[273]

These Elohim-like beings are "retarded Elohim" (*zurückgebliebenen Elohim*) who inspire a kind of thinking in which people adopt thoughts from their ancestors and conventional thoughts that predominate in tribes and communities. It is the impulse of the "abstract divine" (CW 222, *Die Impulsierung des weltgeschichtlichen Geschehens durch geistige Mächte*, March 17, 1923).

The gaze of the author of the *Book of Revelation* now fell on the teaching that arose in the Orient, around 666, and harkens back to the Mysteries that know nothing of the Son: Mohammedanism. The teaching of Mohammedanism only knows the realm of the Father. It knows only the rigid doctrine: there is but one God, besides Him there is nothing, and Mohammed is His prophet. *From this angle* (emphasis by J.v.S.) the teachings of Mohammed are the strongest polarity to Christianity. In them is the will to do away with freedom, the will to bring about determinism, as they represent the world of the Father God. This can only lead to the human being denying his humanness. It is a teaching that has given rise to materialism and its consequence, Darwinism: the ahrimanic opponent of the Son of God. Even today we encounter this in the work of the theologian Adolf von Harnack (1851-1930). In every place in his book *What is Christianity?* where he speaks of the Son, we can safely substitute the word "Father" (CW 346, *The Book of Revelation and the Work of the Priest*, September 11, 1924).

But later came the Mongols, the Turks, the Tatar peoples that fought against the Arabs. These Mongols—from which the Turks are descended—did not have a nature god.²⁷⁴ They had what the human being had in the most ancient times: no attention for nature, but an incredibly deep feeling for a spiritual God, a God one can only comprehend in thought and whom one cannot behold in any way.²⁷⁵ And this extraordinary way of viewing God passed over into Islam. The Turks adopted Islam but changed it to fit their own habits. And while the Mohammedan religion had adopted much from old times, such as the arts and sciences, the Turks threw (*schmissen*) everything out that had to do with art and science—they viewed those as the enemy. The Turks were the terror of the West, the terror for everyone who had adopted Christianity. Many Christians made pilgrimages to the Holy Land, but only after the arrival of the Turks did these journeys become dangerous, for the Turks ill-treated the Christians. That was the reason for the Crusades. Christianity had to be saved from Turkish-style Mohammedanism (CW 353, *Die Geschichte der Menschheit und die Weltanschuungen der Kulturvölker*, March 19, 1924).

Balancing the Picture: Freedom

Although according to Steiner Islam has the tendency to "do away with freedom," Steiner also made statements that aim to show that Islam contains an impulse toward individualization too. This impulse is inspired by the *Archai*, the Spirits of Personality.²⁷⁶

Rudolf Steiner:

> Next, certain personalities belonging to Arabic culture in the Near East are seized by the impulses that proceed as thought impulses from the Archai, the Primal Powers. What is contained in these thought impulses spreads particularly across Africa, Spain and all of western Europe. From this thought impulse the Arabic-Spanish culture arose which, much later, still influenced people such as Galileo (1564-1642), Copernicus (1473-1543) and Spinoza (1632-1677). But at the same time, we also see the effects of the thought impulses from the retarded Elohim, which came to expression in an extreme manner in the Turkish masses that came out of Asia to the West. Yes, in everything we see moving, from the fourth

century on, from West to East and from East to West, until the Turkish conquests, we find the struggle between the impulses of the Archai and those of the retarded Elohim: in the Germanic migrations, the Turks, the Huns and the Crusaders. It is the struggle between the Spirits of Personality (Archai) and the community spirit (retarded Elohim). We see this struggle also in the soul of church father St. Augustine (354-430) (CW 222, *Die Impulsierung des weltgeschichtlichen Geschehens durch geistige Mächte*, March 17, 1923).

Who are these "certain personalities"? In one of his karma lectures Steiner names a number of them:

One was Harun al-Rashid (763-809), the Abassid Caliph in Baghdad, a highly cultured, spiritual individuality who lived at the center of a "great spiritual life" (*grossartiges Geistesleben*). Baghdad was a center where Aristotelian philosophy, natural science and the art of medicine had reached a high level, combined with "oriental imaginations and oriental representations." Compared with this the contemporaneous court of Charlemagne was outright primitive. Other representatives of this high Arabic culture mentioned by Steiner in this lecture are General Tarik who waged war in Spain in 711, and an astrological-astronomical scientist, whose name is not mentioned, at the court of Harun's son, Caliph Al-Mamun (813-833). Steiner also mentions the earlier Omayad Muaviya (Caliph 661-680). About the latter he said:

> Muaviya rules not long after Mohammed. He thus stands entirely within Mohammedanism, within the religious life of Arabism. He is a genuine representative of Mohammedanism at that time, but one of those who are growing away from its hide-bound form and entering into that mode of thought which then, discarding the religious form, appears in the sciences and fine arts in the West. Muaviya is a representative spirit in the first century after Mohammed, but one whose thinking is no longer patterned in absolute conformity with that of Mohammed; he draws his impulse from Mohammed, but only his impulse. He has not yet discarded the religious core of Mohammedanism, but has already led it over into the sphere of thought, of logic (CW 235, *Karmic Relationships*, Vol. I, March 16, 1924).

There is still a third lecture in which Steiner spoke about the tension between predestination and freedom. Here Steiner said that this contradiction (*Widerspruch*) in

Islam—and, according to Steiner, this contradiction also exists in Christianity—is in part resolved (*Heilmittel gegen die Widerspruch*) because Islam knows the Nathan Jesus. The Nathan Jesus is the Jesus described in the Gospel of St. Luke (CW 167, *Gegenwärtiges und Vergangenes im Menschengeiste*, May 23, 1916). We will come back later to Isa in Islam.

Conclusions

Islam (Mohammedanism) is an outspoken Father religion which, because of that nature, leads to the tendency to do away with human freedom. This leads to determinism and fatalism. In this view, Steiner does not deviate from the general view of Islam in his time. It is noteworthy that Steiner does not restrict the Father religion to Islam, but also points to this orientation to the Father in (modern) Christianity.

However, the Father religion as an impulse of the "retarded Elohim" is not the only impulse working in Islam. There is also an impulse of the Spirits of Personality, the Archai. We see the struggle between the community spirit and the Spirits of Personality not only in Islam, but everywhere where East and West meet: also in the Christian Crusaders are the retarded Elohim working. Thus, both in Islam and in Christianity there is the struggle between predestination and freedom. We have seen in chapter 3 that the theologian Friedrich Ulrich also said this in 1912. However, the struggle was decided in favor of the retarded Elohim when the Turkish tribes out of far-away Asia conquered the Arabic-Islamic world. Only then did Islam receive its strong fatalistic character.

In Arabic Islam we recognize both impulses—those of the retarded Elohim and those of the Archai. Steiner showed great respect for a number of Arabic-Islamic Caliphs, such as Harun al-Rashid. He called them "lofty spiritual personalities." As we will see, however, in Steiner's lectures it is not always clear when he spoke of which impulse.

The "Impulse" of Islam, Gondishapur and Sorat

Explanation

The following will serve as an introduction concerning Gondishapur and Sorat. In the year 529, the Christian Byzantine emperor Justinian closed the Greek (pagan) academy of Plato in Athens. The academy in Edessa was also closed. The scholars went into exile in the Sassanid empire, the archenemy of Byzantium, and joined the academies existing there. The academy of Gondishapur was one of the intellectual centers of the Sassanid empire; many works by Greek philosophers were translated into Syrian there (the *lingua franca* of Sassanid scholars).

In 638 the Muslims conquered the Sassanid empire. Many scholars continued their work in the new Muslim context, among others in the *House of Science* in Baghdad, which was founded later under Caliph Al-Mamun in 832. In their turn they translated the Greek philosophers from Syrian into Arabic. During the Mongol invasions in the middle of the thirteenth century Gondishapur was destroyed.

Sorat is a name given by Rudolf Steiner to an anti-Christian impulse which he connected with the number of the beast, 666, from the Book of Revelation.

The Dominant Picture: Islam and the Number of the Beast

Quotations from Steiner:

> The author of the Apocalypse foresaw quite decidedly what was threatening humanity. Christianity will ... become a Christianity shrouded in mist. This will occur in the significant year 666 when what lived in Arabism, in Mohammedanism, sprang up everywhere. Arabism then streamed into Europe, a doctrine that could only lead to a failure to understand the human being in his humanness, because the doctrine of the Father was translated into materialism. It was the ahrimanic opposition to the Son God (CW 346, *The Book of Revelation and the Work of the Priest*, September 11, 1924).

> With Arabism breaking through, the great danger arose that the secret of the sun as the secret of Christ would be forgotten. In the outer deeds of Arabism and Mohammedanism the Sun Demon was working, who opposes the Christian principle in humanity. From this Arabism everything would emerge which would bring the human being closer to the animal. What would have happened if Arabism, the doctrine of the Sun Demon, had been entirely victorious? The Sun Demon only permits the Father principle, with the result that the understanding of transubstantiation[277] would be lost. The name of the Sun Demon is Sorat. He was active for the first time in the year 666, the time when Arabism brought materialism that goes against Christianity. He appeared once more around 1332 (2 x 666), when the Templars were destroyed, and will again appear in 1998 (3 x 666) (CW 346, *The Book of Revelation and the Work of the Priest*, September 12, 1924).

We may wonder what would have happened in the evolution of humanity if Christ had not appeared on earth. Then the number of the beast, 666, would have been victorious. What does this number represent? It represents an incredible wisdom, but a wisdom which humanity was completely unable to bear, because the consciousness soul[278] had not yet awakened. This wisdom would have been bestowed on us whereas we really had to develop it over a long period of time. As a result it becomes "instinct wisdom" (*aus einem Instinkt ... hätten die Menschen ein unreifes Wissen erlangt*). The consequence would have been that humanity would have been unable to develop its higher elements, [279] the spirit; we would have become total "earth beings."

Can we verify this in outer history? We can indeed: in the academy of Gondishapur. When the scholars there translated Aristotle via Syrian into Arabic, the Greek Aristotle became colored in an Arabic soul mood. The Arab soul is remarkable: the sharpest thinking is connected with a certain fantasy (*Phantastik*) that proceeded in logical channels and ascended to the stage of vision. Thus arose the immense world view of Gondishapur.

The ambition of Gondishapur thus became to develop an all encompassing erudition that would have made the human being completely earth-bound, in sharp distinction with the event of Golgotha. It would take the place of the development (*Anstrengungen*) of the consciousness soul and would have diverted humanity from its spiritual development (*Hineinentwickelung in die geistige Welt*). Humanity would have become purely materialistic (CW 184, *Die Polarität von Dauer und Entwickelung im Menschenleben*, October 12, 1918).

Balancing the Picture: Blunting the Influence

Rudolf Steiner:

> But this development proceeding from Gondishapur was held back (*abgestumpft*) by the—in a certain sense—retarding spiritual powers (*retardierende geistigen Kräften*) of Mohammedanism, which still have a connection with what has been influenced by the Christ impulse. At the same time however it is also a kind of antithesis of the Christ impulse. Mohammed spread a fantastic (*phantastische*) religious doctrine exactly over those areas where the Gnostic wisdom of Gondishapur wanted to

penetrate. It is the "wisdom of world history" that Mohammedanism was destined to blunt (*abzustumpfen*) the Gnostic wisdom of Gondishapur, to take away the strong ahrimanic power of temptation.

However, the impulse of Gondishapur did not disappear completely. It is still working in the natural sciences. The blunted Gnostic wisdom came via southern Europe and Africa to Spain, France and England (CW 184, *Die Polarität von Dauer und Entwickelung im Menschenleben*, October 12, 1918).

All wisdom would in this way have been without the Mystery of Golgotha. The development of the consciousness soul would have taken place without the Mystery of Golgotha (CW 184, *Die Polarität von Dauer und Entwickelung im Menschenleben*, October 13, 1918).

Toward the year 666 those scholars gathered in Gondishapur who did not acknowledge the Mystery of Golgotha. They were inspired by luciferic-ahrimanic forces. These extremely learned and brilliant people would have spread over all of western Asia, North-Africa, southern and western Europe. The consciousness soul would have been born too early and the world would have been diverted (*abgebracht*) from the Mystery of Golgotha. But it did not happen that way. Gondishapur's influence was blunted. That which came with Arabic scholars and scientists to Spain was but a shadow of the wisdom of Gondishapur. Mohammedanism took its place. And yet the remainders of the impulse of Gondishapur worked through in, for instance, the Eighth Ecumenical Council of the Catholic Church in 869, when the spirit was "abolished" (CW 182, *Death as Metamorphosis of Life*, October 16, 1918).

Via a detour through Arabism, Aristotle came back to Europe in the Middle Ages. But then people began to study Aristotle without the Greek spirit. The Greeks practiced philosophy with imaginative vision of the spiritual, but the Scholastics no longer had any consciousness of the (Greek) world of ideas. By the closing of the academy of Plato by Justinian, the living connection with such imaginations was broken (CW 74, *The Philosophy of Thomas Aquinas*, May 22, 1920; CW 325, *Die Naturwissenschaft und die weltgeschichtliche Entwickelung der Menschheit seit dem Altertum*, May 16, 1921).

THE IMPULSE OF FREEDOM IN ISLAM

What was it that the Arabic science of Gondishapur wanted to achieve? The science that came to Europe through Averroes (1126-1198) and Avicenna (980-1037) [see chapter 7]. It is the struggle for the consciousness soul that should really have waited until the fifteenth century. It is the struggle for the "I." But for the ancient Greeks this struggle was still accompanied by knowledge from the mysteries, which made the insight possible that the human "I" was not an independent entity (*Wesenheit*) but is fundamentally united with the Divine All. As such, the "I" would be a physical, soul- and spiritual reality. But Avicenna could no longer find those connections. Therefore his picture that the individual soul comes into being only at birth and returns to the Godhead after death (CW 204, *Perspektiven der Menschheitsentwickelung*, June 5, 1921).

The academy of Gondishapur was one of the places where the ancient knowledge had been preserved; it lived there in the form in which Aristotle had been able to teach it. But it was seized by that Oriental stream which one can describe as Arabism. In one aspect of its knowledge, Arabism was a premature unfolding of the consciousness soul. This created the possibility for a spiritual wave to go forth extending over Asia, Africa, southern and western Europe, and filling certain people of Europe with an intellectualism that ought to have come later. In the seventh and eighth centuries, southern and western Europe received spiritual impulses which ought to have come only in the age of the consciousness soul. This spiritual wave was able to awaken the intellectual life in human beings, but not the deeper founts of experience whereby the soul penetrates (*tauchen*) into the world of spirit. Arabism held back the souls of humanity, in knowledge, from the spirit world. It brought the intellect prematurely into activity which was only able to apprehend the outer world of nature. One did feel the world of ideas in oneself and one possessed the tradition of the spirit world, but one was unable to reach it because the soul was impregnated with Arabic intellectualism. In the Middle Ages, realism[280] did know the world of ideas but one could not find its reality. Nominalism, on the other hand, denied the spirit world. Nominalism became the way of thinking of the natural sciences (*Natur-Erkenntnis*) (CW 26, *Anthroposophical Leading Thoughts*, March 1925, V).

Conclusions

In considering the above it is of the greatest importance to make a sharp distinction between Arabism and Mohammedanism. For it really seems as if Steiner sometimes uses these two concepts interchangeably. For instance, when he discusses the Sorat impulse and Gondishapur, he always talks about Arabism, and it is precisely Mohammedanism which blunts this impulse. But in the lecture to the priests of the Christian Community (CW 346, *The Book of Revelation and the Work of the Priest*) Arabism and Mohammedanism are used interchangeably. This creates the impression that both Arabism and Mohammedanism represent the impulse of Gondishapur.

Islam tempered the Sorat impulse of the academy of Gondishapur, but at the same time part of its tempered effect did become part of Islam, which is the reason why Steiner said that "*from this angle* (page 161 above) *the teachings of Mohammed are the strongest polarity to Christianity.*" We will return to this in our discussion of Jesus and Islam.

If the Sorat impulse of the academy of Gondishapur had been able to develop freely, the human being would have been completely cut off from the spirit and the Mystery of Golgotha. This did not happen because Islam blunted its effect. Islam took away the strong ahrimanic temptation. But how? The answer is very surprising: through retarding spiritual powers which nevertheless have a connection with the Christ impulse.

The impulse of the academy of Gondishapur did not entirely disappear. We find it again in the "abolition of the spirit" at the Eighth Ecumenical Council in 869. We find it also in the destruction of the Templars, and then again in 1998 (about which Steiner did not elaborate). We find it in Darwinism (the human being as animal) and in modern (western) natural science.

Rudolf Steiner gave a great deal of attention to this impulse of the academy of Gondishapur. Not all the lectures in which he spoke about it have been mentioned here. I have not been able to find this emphasis and this view of the impulse of Gondishapur in any other source in his time. Evidently, this is a unique insight.

Isa in Islam

Explanation

Rudolf Steiner mentioned Isa in the Koran relatively often—relatively, because it was in his time, and also in ours, not self-evident. Most Christians are not aware of the fact that Isa plays a very important role both in the Koran and in the tradition, but many Muslims do not know this either.

In his Christology Rudolf Steiner distinguishes between two Jesus children: the so-called Solomon Jesus from the Gospel of St. Matthew and the so-called Nathan Jesus from St. Luke. According to Steiner, when the Koran speaks about Jesus, the Nathan Jesus is meant. The only time that Jesus' youth is mentioned in the New Testament is in the Gospel of St. Luke (2:22-40). This lacuna was compensated by a number of apocryphal childhood gospels from the second and third centuries after Christ. Mohammed knew these apocryphal stories (see chapter 4).

The Dominant Picture: Islam Does Not Know Christ

The focus of Islam on the Father God—which is of course also a Christian concept—is in part the consequence of the rejection of Christ as the Son of God. We have already discussed this at length. For this reason, a single quotation from Rudolf Steiner will suffice here:

> Mohammed knew Christianity, but Christianity does not have three gods, but three divine persons: Father, Son and Holy Spirit. Mohammed recognized how the old (Arab) paganism with its many gods had degenerated and would ruin humanity. He saw that Christianity, with its three gods, also harbored that danger, not realizing that these represent three persons of the same one God. Thus he opposed Christianity and emphasized that there is but one God. Islam therefore lacks a representation of the three Divine Persons. Islam views God principally as the Father, the creator who works in nature. And just as a stone or a plant has no free will, in Islam arose a rigid view of destiny: if a human being is happy, it comes from the Father, and similarly when one is unhappy.
>
> The Father works in the nature of our bodies. Spiritual forces work everywhere in nature, and also in our bodies. The spirit of nature is the Father. The Sun Spirit, the Son, does not work in the body but in the human free will that vacillates between good and evil. Then there is the third divinity, the Holy Spirit which sanctifies the will. God therefore reveals Himself in three ways: as a nature god, a god of the will and a spirit god, but they are one (CW 353, *From Beetroot to Buddhism*, March 19, 1924).

Balancing the Picture: the Nathan Jesus

Rudolf Steiner:

> On the one hand Mohammedanism has a strong consciousness of predestination, *kismet*. But on the other hand, Mohammedans say with everything they do: "God willing" (*Inshallah*). That is an insoluble contradiction that is also known to people in the West. All western philosophers are familiar with it. Only, the contradiction is most evident in the doctrine of *kismet*.
>
> If humanity wants to overcome (*hinausgeführt werden*) this contradiction, something has to enter the development of the earth which, while it belongs to the earth, had not incarnated before; something that was held back in ancient Lemurian times[281] when the human being descended. This is the Nathan Jesus, exactly because he remained free of the contradiction and never had anything to do with it. The Nathan Jesus appeared as the remedy for this contradiction. The contradiction is a legacy of the old Zarathustra culture; for this reason the Nathan Jesus had to appear side by side with the Zarathustra Jesus (the Solomon Jesus).[282] And just where the contradiction is strongest, as it is in Mohammedanism, it is there that the revelation of the Nathan Jesus flowed in (*zugeflossen*). When we recognize the nature of the Koran again—that which is revealed to us in the Koran—we will see how there predestination and *inshallah* come together (*zusammenschliessen*). In its current development Mohammedanism has not yet reached that point, but the seed of development is there.
>
> Christians, however, should be beyond that point. Christians should understand who it is who went through the Mystery of Golgotha at the moment when the forces of earth development converged in him. They should (*sollten*) understand how this primeval legacy of humanity came through the Zarathustra nature and that through the Nathan Jesus it received the immediate gift (*unmittelbare Gabe*) of the human (CW 167, *Gegenwärtiges und Vergangenes im Menschengeiste*, May 23, 1916).

These days there are many ministers and priests who cannot understand that Christ—they say Jesus—entered into human evolution in a different way from all other people. They view Jesus as an extraordinary human being, perhaps even the most noble one. Famous theologians speak of the poor (*schlichte*) man Jesus. But can we call such people Christians?

Take someone who says: "Everything that is said about Jesus as Zarathustra and so on goes against my faith. But I hold on to one thing: that the being that lived in Jesus entered into the world in a supernatural way, that this being spoke immediately after his birth—something that others don't do—and that he predicted that he would not die the same kind of death as other people." Then one can say: "This view has accepted only that part of Christianity which is indicated in the Gospel of St. Luke as the Jesus child of the lineage of Nathan."

Let's assume there is a religious document. Then we say: "The one who believes this is influenced by a garbled tradition which can only be straightened out by spiritual-scientific knowledge of the second Jesus child." I will read to you from such a document. [Then the following unidentified quotation is read.]

> *At length she brought the babe to her people, carrying him in her arms. They said: O Mary! truly an amazing thing hast thou brought! O sister of Aaron! Thy father was not a man of evil, nor thy mother a woman unchaste! But she pointed to the babe. They said: How can we talk to one who is a child in the cradle? He said: I am indeed a servant of Allah. He hath given me revelation and made me a prophet; and He hath made me blessed wheresoever I be, and hath enjoined on me Prayer and Charity as long as I live; He hath made me kind to my mother, and not overbearing or miserable; so peace is on me the day I was born, the day that I die, and the day that I shall be raised up to life again!*

In this way this document speaks about Jesus, of whom one representation remains. People who believe this in fact believe more than many who call themselves Christians in our time. Does not someone who stands by this document really believe much more of Christianity? And it is not some small sect that teaches this. I read to you from the Koran.[283] Every real Turk believes this. Many Turks believe more of Christianity than those who call themselves Christians (CW 167, *Gegenwärtiges und Vergangenes im Menschengeiste*, May 16, 1916).

Remember that I read to you from the Koran, and how indeed the Turk who knows his Koran believes much more in Jesus than many modern ministers and priests believe and confess (CW 169, *Toward Imagination*, July 11, 1916).

I would like to know what a Turk would say when a modern Protestant would try to communicate his or her view of Christ, which is really not much more than that Jesus was a remarkable human being. The Turk would say: "Is that your story and you tell me you are a Christian? Read Sura 19—it says much more about Christ than what you are telling me." Indeed, the Turks know much more about Christ Jesus (*Christus Jesus*) than modern pastors. The Koran tells much more about him, and in the Turkish creed Christ Jesus is placed (*herangeführt*) much more in a context of divinity than in the modern protestant creed (CW 172, *Karma of Vocation*, November 27, 1916).

Conclusions

Islam rejects Christ as the Son of God, but Islam does give Isa a very important role in the Koran and in the *hadith* (see chapter 4). Steiner calls this Isa the Nathan Jesus. The statements Steiner made concerning Jesus in the Koran are completely unique.

What is the significance of Isa in the Koran according to Steiner? Islam—and Christianity also—is characterized, among other things, by the tension between predestination/fatalism and freedom. This tension is resolved by Isa, the Nathan Jesus. Jesus is a remedy (*heilmittel*). Precisely in the Koran predestination and freedom flow together, because precisely in the Koran the Nathan Jesus works. That is revealed in the Koran.

Steiner resolutely declares that "Turks" often believe more of Christianity than those who call themselves Christians. Mind the words: in this connection Steiner speaks of Jesus *and* Christ Jesus. Christians who view Christ Jesus primarily as a prophet or simple man are in fact Turks, for Islam does not know the Son of God but it does know the prophet Isa. And that is already more than we can say of Christians.

General Conclusions

In general terms, Rudolf Steiner is not exactly positive about Islam, especially where the character of predestination and fatalism is concerned. This view of Steiner is not noteworthy—it pretty much reflects the general view of imperialist Europe around 1900 (and even today).

THE IMPULSE OF FREEDOM IN ISLAM

According to Steiner, the tendency toward unfreedom is to an important extent determined by the fact that Islam is a Father religion. Islam is oriented on the working of the divine in nature and in the physical human being, but it denies the working of the Son God in the soul. For that matter, in his critique on the orientation on the Father God, Steiner does not limit himself to Islam; things are precisely the same in (modern) Christianity. Steiner is even quite radical: Islam has understood more of Christ Jesus than many modern Christian theologians.

Rudolf Steiner points to the Nathan Jesus in Islam. It is this Isa who is taught by Mohammed, because it is this Jesus who is able to resolve the tension between predestination and freedom.

The strong view of predestination of the Father God in Islam works in the creative nature forces which also work in the physical body of the human being. This can lead to a view of the human being as a purely physical entity and, ultimately, to materialism and Darwinism in the West. Steiner calls this the impulse of the ahrimanic opponent of the Son of God.

But in fact this is not the impulse of Islam. It is the impulse of the academy of Gondishapur where, in the seventh century, the "number of the beast" was working: 666. That is the impulse of Sorat who incites the human being to view himself purely as an animal. It is the academy of Gondishapur that stimulated the extreme Father God orientation.

Mohammedanism has had the effect of tempering this impulse, but it is a pity that Steiner did not specify what it was in Islam that had this tempering effect. He only said that it occurred. He only made one short statement which, right away, has great importance: the development that proceeded from Gondishapur was held back (*abgestumpft*) by the, in a certain sense, retarding spiritual forces of Mohammedanism, forces that have a relationship with what was influenced by the Christ impulse.

It looks as if this refers to the Nathan Jesus. For he tempers the Father God by resolving the tension between predestination and freedom. It is the Nathan Jesus who tempers the Sorat impulse of the academy of Gondishapur. This fits in with the eschatology of Islam, namely that at the end of time Isa will return to defeat the Antichrist (see chapter 4).

Isa is a remedy; he brings the mercy of the human which resolves the tension between predestination and freedom.

But at the same time, Islam adopted elements of Gondishapur and did become a Father religion, only—evidently—not quite as extreme as Sorat had intended. From this point of view Islam is diametrically opposed to the Christianity of the Son but, says Steiner, so is modern Christian theology.

Afterword: Freedom in Islam

Dr. Ibrahim Abouleish
(translated from German by Gertrud K. Kohler)

The Koran says: "Allah does not change the condition of a people until they change their own condition" (Sura 13:11). This is the foundation stone of SEKEM, an Egyptian working community and initiative for sustainable development of humanity, earth and society, founded by Dr. Ibrahim Abouleish.

Freedom can only arise in relation to others. When human beings enter into a connection with Allah, they will find their allotted place on earth (*khalifa*). That is the prerequisite for the human being to be able to develop toward freedom. Allah bestows freedom on human beings, but it is human beings themselves who turn this freedom into unfreedom in the name of religion. Freedom comes into being in the heart, in our deepest self, in the "I." Then the human being experiences oneself as a spiritual being and knows oneself in harmony with the divine spirit in the world.

Human beings are slaves when they follow their natural urges and passions. The way to freedom is the way to the spirit. Freedom has to develop. Freedom does not arise in individuals who isolate themselves; it comes into being in connection with the other, nature and God. Islam is a search for that connection with the human community (*umma*), with the creation of Allah. That is the way taught by the Koran. How? By following the Koran, by meditating on the Koran, and by spiritual scientific research (*ijtihad*) into the Koran.

Freedom is the human being's most precious possession. One can only develop oneself in freedom. Freedom is not an abstract concept which has the same meaning in all places and at all times. For a child freedom has a different meaning than for an adult. However, both need freedom so they can develop their abilities. A society also needs freedom to realize itself as a collective. Freedom is diverse.

The highest human ideal in Islam is the development of human beings to become the representatives of Allah on earth (*khalifa*). They live in the consciousness that God has created them and that they should read and recognize the signs of God in the world surrounding them. When they enter into a relationship with Allah in such a way that they recognize Him as their creator, they find their allotted place in the world. This is a prerequisite for their development toward freedom.

The freedom a mother grants her child can only be that freedom which is appropriate for the child within the framework of its understanding and development. The freedom Allah grants to human beings can only realize itself when human beings know themselves as beings that have their place in the Universe solely in relation to the Most High. Even someone who thinks freedom only exists when human beings take it, or even win it by force, will realize that freedom only makes sense when human beings are able to bring their spirits into relation with the Spirit of the World. If they do not do that, they are either imprisoned in themselves or they are a slave of nature. They are then not free.

Allah grants freedom, because human beings are created for freedom and Allah is their creator. Allah does not dictate to human beings what to do, he gives them the freedom to develop themselves as human beings, even though Allah has the power to make them subservient to him or punish them. Where human beings are made unfree in the name of religion, this is done by other human beings and not by the divine power itself.

The fact that in the Occident the concept of freedom went hand in hand with secularization, liberation from religion is part of the character of western cultural development. In the Orient the path is different. Here the experience of freedom does not occur through overturning outer institutions; instead it has its source in the heart. Many people in the West also knew and lived this, starting with the Mystics, continuing with the philosophers of Idealism, down to Goethe. Someone who wins freedom in one's Ego experiences oneself as a spiritual being and knows oneself to be in harmony with the divine Spirit of the World.

Sura 2:256 says: "There is no compulsion in religion." This sentence does not mean that you can do whatever you feel like. Religion is not a conglomerate of things people like to do in the name of God, nor is it a compendium of fixed rules of what one must do. To be free of compulsion means that human beings can find the right way in themselves that leads the "spiritual in the human being to the spiritual in the universe," as formulated by Rudolf Steiner. This path can only be found in freedom, but those who tread it can be sure that they will receive help. At that moment, when human beings identify themselves completely with that with which they are united in their innermost heart, they experience the divine as a helping, freedom furthering force.

This divine force acts in Providence. Goethe expressed it in beautiful words: "The moment one decides to dedicate oneself to a task, Providence also stirs. All sorts of things which would otherwise never have happened will now happen to help one. Through this decision a whole stream of events is set in motion which provides for countless unexpected events, encounters and material help which no one could have dreamt of before. Whatever you can do, start it. Boldness bears genius, power and magic. Start now."

The divine can never work through compulsion. Human beings are the ones who force each other to opinions and deeds in the name of God. Those who are forced to accept religion close their hearts to the Divine; then they cannot approach the Divine. There are human beings who are touched by the Divine, shaken or even overcome by it, because the experience is so powerful. However, no one will ever experience this as compulsion; as a matter of fact it is the opposite—it is an experience of liberation.

Everything undergoing a process of development always retains something of the same. A plant always remains a plant, even while being a seed, germinating, bringing forth leaves and blossoming. But this constant element is not visible, because we always see only a stage of development. Goethe experienced this and called it the archetypal plant (*Urpflanze*). Even in SEKEM, where there is so much in development, something always stays the same; it is the vision of SEKEM that always shows itself in a particular manifestation. This constant element in all things is of a spiritual nature, and even though it is diverse, as a constant it is always one. Human beings are called upon to see this constant element in the phenomena of nature. The Koran calls this: reading in the book of nature and recognizing the signs of Allah.

Sura 96 is the first revealed Sura. In the first verse the angel Gabriel speaks to Mohammed: "Read in the name of your Lord, who created" (Sura 96:1). If human beings can read the signs of God, that is, if they can recognize that which is constant in the appearances, they become free in relation to nature, and can develop culture and civilization. Then they can form the life of the community in a manner that is worthy of the human being. Knowing the Divine in nature means knowing the laws of nature in the physical world; knowing the laws of life (formative forces) in the organic world; and in the spiritual world knowing the deeds of the beings themselves. If we know them we can work together with them, and thus freedom comes into being.

Freedom is not separation from everything; on the contrary, it is a joining, a cooperating with the Divine in nature and in humanity. Therefore, to freedom also belongs responsible handling of nature and its sustainable ecological treatment. People cannot be forced to do this. The Koran says again and again that Allah leaves it up to human beings which way they want to go or not go, and also that human beings may not say, once called to judgment, that they did not know. For instance, Sura 18:29 says: "And say: The truth is from your Lord, so let them who please believe, and let them who please disbelieve."

Allah does not interfere, even though he could: "And if We had pleased We would certainly have given to every soul its guidance" (Sura 32:13). Allah gives human beings the freedom to treat the earth respectfully. The will has to come from human beings. But Islam also knows this means that human beings were given a huge task. The Koran expresses this in a powerful picture: "Surely We offered the trust to the heavens and the earth and the mountains, but they refused to be unfaithful to it and feared from it, and humans have turned unfaithful to it; surely they are unjust, ignorant" (Sura 33:72). The world and humanity have a common destiny, but human beings have the freedom to face this destiny and develop the world further.

When the Koran says that the human being has taken on the responsibility for the world, this means also that the future of the world lies in the human being. In other words: the future of the macrocosm lies in the microcosm. In every individual human being lies the key for the world to receive more human dignity and become more God-like. For this, education is needed. If human beings are educated in a free manner they will be able to carry their responsibility for the world.

This creates a cycle of freedom. Human beings experience themselves and nature as God's creation. They are called upon to read this creation. They thereby receive the ability to transform nature. By doing this they further enliven nature and develop themselves. This impulse is possible all over the world, anywhere and any time.

Notes

1. Sura 48:21.
2. Sura 3:145.
3. Sura 13:11.
4. Sura 53:39.
5. Sura 30:30.
6. Sura 2:256.
7. In the Koran we encounter Iblis (the devil) for the first time in the company of the angels. In traditional exegesis the assumption was always made that Iblis was a *jinn*, a spirit created from fire that dwelled among the angels because of his high knowledge. He was not a fallen angel as is presumed in other sources (Sura 18:50). Angels can do only what God tells them to do (Sura 16:49-50), but Iblis has his own ideas. The Koran does not describe Iblis as an anti-god, for God has no opposite, but perhaps more as anti-human or anti-angel. Traditionally, this whole story is regarded as a metaphor for the battle between good and evil.
8. Sura 2:30-39.
9. Sura 7:16; 15:39; 17:62; 38:82.
10. Sura 15:26-49.
11. Sura 7:17.
12. Sura 7:172.
13. Sura 2:35; 7:19.
14. Sura 20:120.
15. Sura 18:7.
16. Sura 18:29.
17. Sura 5:48.
18. Sura 10:99.
19. Abu Yusuf, Kitab al-Kharaj.
20. Sura 2:62.
21. Sura 95:8.
22. Sura 109:6.
23. Sura 88: 21-22.

24 Sura 27:92.
25 Sura 17:70.
26 E. W. Said, *Orientalism*, New York, 1978.
27 K. May, *Im Sudan*.
28 Ibid.
29 Ibid.
30 K. May, *Durchs Wilde Kurdistan*, Karl-May-Verlages, first edition 1881.
31 K. May, *Von Bagdad nach Stambul*, Karl-May-Verlages, first edition 1882.
32 Ibid.
33 *Die Grosse Politik der Europaeischen Kabinette 1871-1914*.
34 M. S. Abdullah, *Geschichte des Islams in Deutschland*, Graz, Vienna, Cologne, 1981.
35 H. Weiss, "German Images of Islam in West Africa," *Sudanic Africa*, 11/2000; G. Hagen, "German Heralds of Holy War: Orientalist and Applied Oriental Studies," *Comparative Studies of South Asia, Africa and the Middle East*, 24:2 (2004).
36 C. Mirbt, *Mission und Kolonialpolitik*, Tuebingen, 1910.
37 G. H. Weiss, Op. cit.
38 For Goethe see: Hajj Abu Bakr Rieger, *Goethe Embraced Islam*, Weimar, 1995; K. Mommsen, *Goethe und der Islam*, Frankfurt am Main, 2001; W. F. Veltman, *Goethe en Europa. Een bezinning op de huidige wereldsituatie*, Zeist, 1982.
39 Goethe, *Letter to Schlosser*, Weimarer Ausgabe IV, 25.
40 Goethe, *Die West-Östliche Divan*, Weimarer Ausgabe I, 6.
41 Goethe, *Letter to Willemer*, Weimarer Ausgabe IV, 34.
42 T. Nöldeke, *Geschichte des Qorans*, Göttingen, 1860.
43 I. Warraq, "A Personal Look at Some Aspects of the History of Koranic Criticism in the Nineteenth and Twentieth Centuries," K-H. Ohlig and G-R. Puin (eds.), *Die dunklen Anfänge. Neue Forschungen zur Entstehung und frühen Geschichte des Islams*, Verlag Hans Schiller, 2005; M. Frenschkowski, "Wellhausen," *Biographisch-Bibliographisches Kirchenlexikon*, part XIII (1998).
44 See for instance: E. Mulder and T. Milo, *De omstreden bronnen van de islam*, Zoetermeer, 2009.
45 Weber makes frequent use of F. Ulrich, *Die Vorherbestimmungslehre im Islam und Christentum*.
46 See W. Schluchter, "Hindrances to Modernity: Max Weber on Islam," T. Huff and W. Schluchter, *Max Weber and Islam*, New Brunswick/London, 1999.
47 See J. L. M. van Schaik, *Unde Malum. Dualisme bij manicheers en katharen. Een vergelijkend onderzoek*, Kampen, 2004.
48 J. Calvin, *Institutes of the Christian Religion*, Library of Christian Classics.
49 G. Oussani, "Mohammed and Mohammedanism," *Catholic Encyclopedia*, part X, 1911.
50 L. R. Conradi, *Mystery Unfolds or The Seven Seals Opened*.
51 Ibid.

52. Ibid.
53. Among others: *Halley's Bible Handbook with the New International Version*, 2000.
54. L. R. Conradi, Op. cit.
55. Ibid.
56. Ibid.
57. Oussani, *Mohammed and Mohammedanism*.
58. S. Cranston, *H. P. B.: The Extraordinary Life and Influence of Helena Blavatsky, Founder of the Modern Theosophical Movement*, Pasadena, 1995.
59. Published in *The Sun*, New York, Vol. XLII, #111, January 2, 1876, *Collected Writings Online*, Vol. I.
60. H. P. Blavatsky, *Collected Writings Online, The Secret Doctrine*.
61. A. Besant, "The Brotherhood of Religions," *Adyar Pamphlets*, #24, 1919.
62. A. Besant, *Beauties of Islam*, Adyar, 2002.
63. N. Baig Mirza, *Reincarnation and Islam*, Adyar, 1996.
64. C. G. Harrison, *The Transcendental Universe. Six Lectures on Occult Science, Theosophy and Catholic Faith*, London, 1993.
65. Rudolf Steiner probably used this book when he made his remark on the Islamic paradise. See R. Steiner, *Grundelemente der Esoterik*, GA 93A, Dornach, 1987.
66. R. Steiner, *Apocalypse en priesterschap*, GA 346, Zeist, 2005 (English edition: *The Book of Revelation and the Work of the Priest*, London, 1998).
67. R. Steiner, *The Book of Revelation and the Work of the Priest*, GA 346, London, 1998, September 11, 1924.
68. R. Steiner, *Gegenwaertiges and Vergangenes im Menschengeiste*, GA 167, May 23, 1916, not available in English (translated by Philip Mees).
69. See R. Steiner, *Die Impulsierung des weltgeschichtlichen Geschehens durch geistige Maechte*, GA 222, March 17, 1923; see also part 4: *Rudolf Steiner on Islam*.
70. R. Steiner, *From Beetroot to Buddhism ...*, GA 353, lectures to workers, March 19, 1924.
71. R. Steiner, *Gegenwaertiges und Vergangenes im Menschengeiste*, GA 167, May 23, 1916.
72. Ibid., May 16, 1916.
73. Ibid.
74. R. Steiner, *The Book of Revelation and the Work of the Priest*, GA 346, London, 1998, September 11, 1924.
75. G. I. Gurdjieff, *Meetings with Remarkable Men* (Autobiography), London, 1972; W. J. Hanegraaff (ed.), *Dictionary of Gnosis and Western Esotericism*, Part 1, 2005.
76. J. Slomp, *De Soefi Beweging*, Kampen, 2007; A. Schimmel, *Gabriel's Wing. A Study into the Religious Ideas of Sir Mohammad Iqbal*, Leiden, 1963.
77. J. Slomp, *De Soefi Beweging*, Kampen, 2007; A. Rawlinson, "A History of Western Sufism," *Diskus*, Vol. I, nr. 1 (1993).

78 Modern researchers wonder whether the story of the four honorable Caliphs is not more legend than reality. See E. Mulder and T. Milo, *De omstreden bronnen van de islam*, Zoetermeer, 2009.
79 W. Raven, *Ibn Ishaak. Het Leven van Mohammed*, Amsterdam, 2000.
80 Ibid.
81 See K.-H. Ohlig and G.-R. Puin, *Die dunklen Anfänge: Neue Forschungen zur Entstehung und frühen Geschichte des Islam*, Schiller Verlag, 2005; also Mulder and Milo, Op. cit.
82 H. Kennedy, *The Great Arab Conquest. How the Spread of Islam Changed the World We Live In*, Weidenfeld and Nicolson, 2007.
83 Chr. Luxenberg, *Neudeutung der arabische Inschrift im Felsendom zu Jerusalem*, Ohlig and Puin, Op. cit.
84 Ibid. Much more could be said about this inscription. For instance, the word "Islam" was not yet a proper name but meant "agreement (with God)." C. Luxenberg, *Neudeutung der arabischen Inschrift im Felsendom zu Jerusalem*, Ohlig and Puin, Op. cit.
85 The Sharif was the protector of the holy places of the Hashemites of the family of Mohammed.
86 F. Ulrich, *Die Vorherbestimmungslehre im Islam und Christentum: eine religionsgeschichtliche Parallele*, Bertelsmann, 1912.
87 S. M. Zwemer, *Islam, A Challenge to Faith: Studies on the Mohammedan Religion and the Needs and Opportunities of the Mohammedan World from the Standpoint of Christian Mission*, New York, 1907.
88 R. Steiner, *Karmic Relationships*, Vol I, GA 235, London, 1955, March 16, 1924.
89 I. Goldziher, *Vorlesungen über den Islam*, Heidelberg, 1925.
90 F. Ulrich, Op. cit.
91 Ibid.
92 Ibid.
93 Ibid.
94 R. Steiner, *Gegenwärtiges und Vergangenes im Menschengeiste*, GA 167 (not available in English), May 23, 1916.
95 R. Steiner, *Karmic Relationships*, Vol I, GA 235, London, 1955, March 16, 1924.
96 R. Steiner, *The Driving Force of Spiritual Powers on World History*, GA 222, March 17, 1923.
97 Ibid.
98 R. Steiner, *The Archangel Michael, His Mission and Ours*, November 28, 1919, from GA 194.
99 J. van Schaik, *Westerse esoterie en oosterse wijsheid. De esoterische traditie door de eeuwen heen*, Kampen, 2010.
100 Monumenta Germaniae Historica, Conc. III, 183.
101 A. Diem, *Een verstoorder van de "ordo," Gottschalk van Orbais en zijn leer van de dubbele predestinatie*, in the book: M. de Jong, M. T. Bos, and C. van Rhijn, *Macht en gezag in de negende eeuw*, Hilversum, 1995.
102 Anselmus, *De libertate arbitrii*.

NOTES

103   A. Th. Khoury, *Der Koran*, Düsseldorf, 2005.
104   S. M. Azmayesh and J. van Schaik, *Een ontmoeting met Jezus in christendom en islam*, Kampen, 2008.
105   A. van Bommel, *Kom tot het gebed: Een korte inleiding tot de praktijk van de islam*, The Hague, n.d.
106   http://en.wikipedia.org/wiki/Basmala
107   H.-J. Klimheit, *Gnosis on the Silk Road. Gnostic Parables, Hymns and Prayers from Central Asia*, San Francisco, 1993.
108   See *Encyclopaedia of Islam*, New Edition, Vol. VIII, Leiden, 1995; also H.-J. Klimheit, Op. cit.
109   For this paragraph see R. Bezertinov, *Tengrianizm—Religion of Turks and Mongols*, Naberezhnye Chelny, 2000.
110   *Encyclopaedia of Islam*, Vol. III.
111   Source: http://www.ghazali.org/books/md/gz101.
112   Al-Ghazali, *Ihya'ul ulum al-din*, transl. N. Amin Faris, *The Book of Knowledge*, Lahore, 1962.
113   Al-Ghazali, *Tahafut al-falasifa*, transl. S. Ahmad Kamali, *The Incoherence of the Philosophers*, Lahore, 1963.
114   Ibid.
115   Al-Ghazali, *The Alchemy of Happiness*, Transl. C. Field, London, 2001.
116   J. van Schaik, *In het hart is Hij te vinden. Een geschiedenis van de christelijke mystiek*, Zeist, 2005.
117   Bernardus de Clairvaux, *Epistolae*, 191, Dunkirk, 1973 (translated from Dutch by Philip Mees).
118   N. Robinson, *Christ in Islam and Christianity. The Representation of Jesus in the Quran and the Classical Muslim Commentaries*, London, 1991.
119   A. Schimmel, *In the Naam van God de Erbarmer, de Barmhartige. Een inleiding in de islam*, Zoetermeer, 1997.
120   N. Robinson, Op. cit.
121   H. Bronkhorst, H. Hagoort and P. Siebesma, *Een Heilige Stad: Jeruzalem in jodendom, christendom en islam*, Leiden, 1996.
122   Bukhari, *Images of Jesus Christ in Islam*, transl. O. Leirvik, Uppsala, 1999.
123   N. Robinson, Op. cit.
124   Bukhari, Op. cit.
125   N. Robinson, Op. cit.
126   N. Robinson, Op. cit.
127   N. Robinson, Op. cit.
128   P. W. van der Horst, *Het Boek der Hemelse Paleizen (3 Enoch). Een joods mystiek geschrift uit de late oudheid*, Kampen, 1999.

129 N. A. Zayd, *Rethinking the Quran. Towards a Humanistic Hermeneutics*, Utrecht, 2004; also N. Robinson, Op. cit.
130 N. Robinson, Op. cit.
131 J. D. Sahas, *John of Damascus on Islam*, Leiden, 1972; also N. Robinson, Op. cit.
132 See E. Mulder and T. Milo, *De omstreden bronnen van de islam*, Zoetermeer, 2009.
133 Ibid.
134 Azmayesh and Van Schaik, *Een ontmoeting met Jezus in christendom en islam*; M. Clark, *Islam for Dummies*, Nijmegen, 2004.
135 T. Khalidi, *Woorden ven Jezus in de moslimtraditie*, Deventer, 2003.
136 Al-Azraqi in F. Wuestenfeld, *Chroniken der Stadt Mekka*, Leipzig, 1858; reprint Beirut, 1964.
137 Raven, *Ibn Ishaak, Het leven van Mohammed*.
138 http://www.tonyburke.ca/infancy-gospel-of-thomas/the-childhood-of-the-saviour-infancy-gospel-of-thomas-a-new-translation/ (transl. Tony Burke 2009)
139 Raven, Op. cit. (translated by Philip Mees).
140 Azmayesh and Van Schaik, Op. cit.
141 Khalidi, Op. cit.
142 Ibid.
143 N. Robinson, Op. cit.
144 Khalidi, Op. cit.
145 Ibid.
146 Ibid.
147 N. Robinson, Op. cit.
148 M. Al-Bahay, *Muhammad Abduh. Eine Untersuchung seiner Erziehungsmethode zum Nationalbewusstsein und zur nationalen Erhebung in Ägypten*, Hamburg, 1936; A. Hourani, *Arabic Thought in the Liberal Age, 1798-1939*, Cambridge, 1983.
149 At that time a well-known mystical brotherhood with many adherents.
150 In Sufism, life is imagined as a long road toward union with God, a road that encompasses several phases and is traveled by gathering knowledge, among other things.
151 C. C. Adams, *Islam and Modernism in Egypt*, 1933; Hourani (Op. cit.) writes: "from the bonds of literalism to the freedom of the true belief in God."
152 Now Azhar University, this school was founded in 970; it has a famous theological faculty that has great authority in the Islamic world.
153 See N. J. Coulson, *A History of Islamic Law*, Edinburgh, 1994.
154 Al-Afghani presented himself on his travels as an Afghan to avoid being rejected as a Shiite. See R. Peters, *Erneuerungsbewegungen im Islam vom 18. bis zum 20. Jahrhundert und die Rolle des Islams in der neuere Geschichte: Antikolonialismus and Nationalismus*, "Der Islam in der Gegenwart," Munich, 1984.
155 C. C. Adams, Op. cit.

NOTES

156 Abu 'Abdullah Muhammad ibn Idris al-Shafi'i (767-820) was a Muslim jurist who is considered the founder of Islamic jurisprudence. According to his generally accepted theory, a judgment in law must be based on the four roots (*usul*) of law: 1. the Koran, 2. the *sunna*, 3. consensus, 4. analogy. Consulting the consensus of the community and reasoning by analogy of other passages in the Koran and the *sunna* were called *ijtihad*, interpretation. See also Coulson, Op. cit.
157 R. Peters, Op. cit.
158 C. C. Adams, Op. cit.
159 Ibid.
160 Hourani, Op. cit.
161 Ibid.
162 A. Lufti al-Sayyid, *Egypt and Cromer: A Study in Anglo-Egyptian Relations*, London, 1968.
163 Sura 13:11.
164 Al-Bahay, Op. cit.
165 See M. H. Kerr, *Islamic Reform: The Political and Legal Theories of Mohammad Abduh and Rashid Rida*, Berkeley and Los Angeles, 1966; and Al-Bahay, Op. cit.
166 Kerr, Op. cit.
167 But this does not mean democracy, writes Kerr. Abduh did not mind if part of the people, e.g., the lowest working class, would not be informed, because they would have the function of mute instruments, restricted to physical activities. Kerr, Op. cit.
168 Al-Bahay, Op. cit.
169 Ibid.
170 Lufti al-Sayyid, Op. cit.
171 Positivism is a philosophy of science based on the view that in the social as well as natural sciences, information derived from sensory experience, logical and mathematical treatments and reports of such data, are together the exclusive source of all authoritative knowledge.... Auguste Comte argued that society operates according to its own quasi-absolute laws, much as the physical world operates according to gravity and other absolute laws of nature. (Source: Wikipedia)
172 Abduh, *Der Islam und die islamische Frage* (*Journal Parisien*, 1899), quoted by Al-Bahay, Op. cit. (translated by Philip Mees).
173 Different English translations carry different titles, including *The Philosophy of Freedom, The Philosophy of Spiritual Activity*, and *Intuitive Thinking as a Spiritual Path*, GA 4.
174 R. Bremmer, L. ten Kate and E. Warrink (eds.), *Encyclopedie van de filosofie van de Oudheid tot vandaag*, Amsterdam, 2007; H. J. Störig, *Geschiedenis van de filosofie 2*, Utrecht, 1988.
175 Rudolf Steiner, *Intuitive Thinking as a Spiritual Path*, GA 4, Great Barrington, MA, 1995.
176 Ibid.
177 Ibid.
178 Ibid.

179   Ibid.
180   Ibid.
181   Ibid.
182   Ibid.
183   W. M. Watt, *Free Will and Predestination in Early Islam*, London, 1948.
184   Ibid.
185   See chapter 3.
186   M. Abduh, *Risalat al Tawhid*, Cairo, 1897.
187   M. Abduh, *The Theology of Unity*, London, 1966, translation of *Risalat al Tawhid* by Msaad and Craig, p. 31: "Such was the way of God in days gone by and you will find it does not change" (Sura 48:23).
188   M. Abduh, *Risalat al Tawhid*, Cairo, 1897: *yashhudu anhu mudrik* (witnesses that he is intelligent, rational) *li amalihi ilikhtiyariyya* (in his voluntary deeds).
189   In this way, faith is therefore also an intuition.
190   M. Abduh, *The Theology of Unity*, London, 1966.
191   Ibid.
192   Ibid.
193   Ibid.
194   M. Abduh, ibid. Abu Hanifa and St. Augustine said approximately the same thing, see G. G. Schojaie, *Das Problem der Freiheit und Determinismus im Islam. Versuch eines Vergleiches mit der abendlaendischen Philosophie*, Munich, 1975.
195   See also the section *Thinking about Freedom* in part 3.
196   M. Abduh, *The Theology of Unity*, London, 1966.
197   Ibid.
198   Abduh makes conscious use here of the double meaning of the word *hasan*, "good" but also "beautiful." See Kerr, Op. cit.
199   M. Abduh, *The Theology of Unity*, London, 1966.
200   Ibid.
201   Ibid.
202   Ibid.
203   Ibid.
204   Ibid., page 107: "Mind submits to the doctrines and rules of conduct that religion discloses. How then can reason be denied its right, being, as it is, the scrutineer of evidences so as to reach the truth within them and know that it is divinely given?"
205   Ibid., page 108: "it is then free to seek ...," and *Risalat al Tawhid*, Cairo, 1987.
206   Ibid.
207   M. Abduh, *Risalat al Tawhid*, Cairo, 1897.
208   M. Abduh, *The Theology of Unity*, London, 1966.
209   Ibid.

210 The divine union or unification, the union of God or the faith in one God—monotheism—is what the verb *wahhada*, which is derived from *tawhid*, wants to express. It includes movement. You could say: God is not one, the faithful makes Him one. In faith the human being plays an active role.

211 O. Scharbrodt, "The Salafiyya and Sufism: Muhammad Abduh and his *Risalat al-Waridat* (Treatise on Mystical Inspirations)," *Bulletin of SOAS*, 70, 1 (2007). London: School of Oriental and African Studies: "Aware of Abduh's musical inclinations Afghani enriched his mysticism with a philosophical underpinning and thereby drew him to a more rationalist interpretation of Islam. Afghani's lessons intellectualized his Sufism with the theosophic tradition of Iranian Shiism. The *Risalat al-Waridat*, written in 1874, reflects the Sufi instructions of Afghani and exhibits the philosophical and esoteric traditions of Islam which had been marginalized in Sunni Islam but had been kept alive within Shiism." In *Risalat al-Waridat* Abduh presents a neo-platonic cosmology and emanation theology.

212 F. Vahdat, "Post-revolutionary Islamic modernity in Iran: The intersubjective hermeneutics of Mohamad Mojtahed Shabestari," S. Taji-Farouki and B.M. Nafi (eds.), *Islamic Thought in the Twentieth Century*, London/New York, 2004: "The usual metaphor that these previous thinkers advanced was that of the "drop in the ocean," whereby the drop disappears in the ocean at the end of the process of theomorphic journey. In Shabestari's ontology, however, not only is this outcome avoided, but the result of the movement toward the Absolute is the affirmation of the human."

213 Henry Corbin (1903-1978) was my great guide into the world of Iranian philosophy and thinking of the spirit. Ever since 1972 I have again and again consulted his works. To learn more about this exceptional figure, see Tom Cheetham's book *The World Turned Inside Out. Henry Corbin and Islamic Mysticism*, Woodstock, 2003.

214 Mohammed Abduh (1849-1905), Egyptian thinker, mystic, journalist and fighter for human rights. In his book *Risalat al Tawhid* (Theology of Unity) he interprets, among other things, the emancipation movements in Europe as the European peoples finding the right track, i.e., the track to Islam. See also chapters 5 and 6.

215 Sura 19:34: "... Isa, son of Maryam; this is the saying of truth...."

216 K. Mommsen, *Goethe und die arabische Welt*, Frankfurt am Main, 1988, later published as *Goethe und der Islam*, Frankfurt am Main, 2001.

217 S. H. Nasr, *The Islamic Intellectual Tradition in Persia*, ed. by M. A. Razavi, Curzon Press, 1996.

218 Avicenna, *Metafisica*, edited by Olga Lizzini and Pasquale Porro, Milan, 2006.

219 S. H. Nasr, "Mulla Sadra: His Teachings," S. H. Nasr and O. Leaman (eds.), *History of Islamic Philosophy*, London, 1996, pp. 643-652 (brief summary of Molla Sadra's thinking).

220 M. H. Yazdi, *The Principles of Epistemology in Islamic Philosophy: Knowledge by Presence*, New York, 1992.

221 Ibid.

222 In the Cartesian paradigm reality is divided into a subjective and objective dimension. In the subjective dimension I exercise the activity of thinking: the "I think" of Descartes. The objective dimension is that to which this thinking is related. Both worlds must be strictly separated and distinguished from each other to guarantee the scientific character of philosophical discourse.

223 With the final result of deconstruction and post-modernism in which there is neither subject nor object left (see Foucault, Derrida, the French post-modernists, and also the Frankfurt School with Popper and Habermas).

224 *Al-haqq* means: reality in the absolute sense of divine origin. *Al-haqq* is therefore also used to indicate God. *Al-haqiqat* is a derivation of this; it means: that which this divine reality represents.

225 M. A. Razavi, *Sohrawardi and the School of Illumination*, Richmond, 1997.

226 A. Soroush, *De betekenis en essentie van secularisme* in the book *Andere berichten uit Teheran. Iraanse identiteit na het fundamentalisme*, Amsterdam, 2000 (translated by Philip Mees).

227 Ibid.

228 S. H. Nasr, *Knowledge and the Sacred*, New York, 1989.

229 S. Nusseibeh, *Avicenna: Providence and God's Knowledge of Particulars* in the book *Avicenna and his Legacy. A Golden Age of Science and Philosophy*, Turnhout, 2009.

230 Avicenna, *Metafisica*, X, 4, 5.

231 H. Motzki, *Het ontstaan van het islamitische recht* in the book: H. Driessen (ed.), *In het huis van de islam. Geografie, geschiedenis, geloofsleer, cultuur, economie, politiek*, Nijmegen, 1997.

232 R. Shah-Kazemi, *Justice and Remembrance, Introducing the spirituality of Imam Ali, The discourse to Kumayl*, I.B.Tauris Publishers, London-New York.

233 His actual name was Abu Ali ibn Sina (980-1037).

234 Y. Tzivi Langermann, foreword in *Avicenna and his Legacy: A Golden Age of Science and Philosophy*, Turnhout, 2009.

235 Sura 89: 27, 28.

236 H. Corbin, *Avicenne et le recit visionnaire*, Verdier, 1999.

237 H. Corbin, *En Islam iranien: Aspects spirituels et philosophiques*, Paris, 1971-1972, and *Histoire de la philosophie islamique*, Paris, 1986.

238 As I later noticed, I wrote this page on July 29—2008!

239 Michael Shepherd (ed.), *Friend to Mankind—Marsilio Ficino (1433-1499)*, London, 1999.

240 Cf. D. van Bemmelen, *Zarathustra: De eerste profeet van Christus*, Zeist, 1967.

241 H. Corbin, *Terre celeste et corps de Resurrection, de l'Iran Mazdeen a l'Iran Shi'ite*, Paris, 1960.

242 *Xvarna* is what makes the soul whole. It works in the region of the soul in the same way in which the World Saviour works in the cosmos.

243 D. van Bemmelen, Op. cit.

244 H. Corbin, *L'homme de lumiere dans le soufisme iranien*, Paris, 1961; S. Hossein Nasr, *The Spread of the Illuminationist School of Sohrawardi. Studies in Comparative Religion*, Vol. 6, No. 3 (Summer 1972), www.studiesincomparativereligion.com.

NOTES

245 S. Y. Sohrawardi, *Kitab Hikmat al-Ishraq: Le livre de la sagesse orientale*, translated and annotated by H. Corbin, Paris, 1986.
246 H. Corbin, *L'Archange empourpre: Quinze recits et traits mystiques de Sohrawardi*, Paris, 1976.
247 The word for vermillion red is *kermesh*.
248 H. Corbin, *L'homme de lumiere dans le Sufism iranien*, Paris, 1972.
249 N. A. Isfaranyini, *"Kashf al-Asrar." Le revelateur des Mysteres*, Paris, 2000.
250 W. C. Chittick, *The Self-Disclosure of God: Principles of Ibn-Arabi's Cosmology*, Albany, 1998.
251 N. Ardalan and L. Bakhtiar, *The Sense of Unity: The Sufi Tradition in Persian Architecture*, Chicago, 1973.
252 M. Ibn Arabi, *La sagesse des prophetes*, Paris, 2008; R. L. Nettler, *Sufi Metaphysics and the Quranic Prophets*, Cambridge, 2003.
253 For an extensive description of the teaching of the Twelve Imams see C. Gruwez, *God is een kleur: Ontmoetingen met het onbekende Iran*, Gent, 2008.
254 G. Jambet, *L'acte d'etre, la philosophie de la Revelation chez Molla Sadra*, Fayard, 2002.
255 M. S. Shirazi, *Le livre des penetrations metaphysiques*, tr. Henry Corbin, Paris, 1988; M. S. Shirazi, *On the Hermeneutics of the Light Verse of the Qu'ran*, tr. L.-P. Peerwani, London, 2004.
256 M. S. Shirazi, *Le livre des penetrations metaphysiques*, tr. Henry Corbin, Paris, 1988.
257 Ibid.
258 See O. Scharmer, *Theory U. Leading from the Future as it Emerges: The Social Technology of Presencing*; and P. Senge, *Presence: An Exploration of Profound Change in People, Organizations and Society*.
259 M. H. Yazdi, *The Principles of Epistemology in Islamic Philosophy: Knowledge by Presence*, New York, 1992.
260 C. Gruwez, "Presence is a deed. Otto Scharmer, Rudolf Steiner and Mehdi Yazdi," *Logos, Onderzoek van de Geest*, Jaarboek, 2010, Kamerling.
261 M. H. Yazdi, *The Principles of Epistemology in Islamic Philosophy: Knowledge by Presence*, New York, 1992.
262 See also the afterword by Dr. Ibrahim Abouleish.
263 A. Soroush, *De betekenis en essentie van secularisme* in the book *Andere berichten uit Teheran. Iraanse identiteit na het fundamentalisme*, Amsterdam, 2000.
264 H. Marcuse and D. Kellner, *One-Dimensional Man: Studies in the Ideology of Advanced Industrial Society*, 1991.
265 J.-J. Rousseau, *Du contrat social*, 1762.
266 See chapter 2.
267 Ghazali, *Le Tabernacle des Lumieres (Michkat Al-Anwar)*, tr. R. Deladriere, Paris, 1981.
268 Ghazali, *La revivification des sciences de la religion (Ihya Ulum al-Din)*, tr. E. de Vitray-Meyerovitch, Paris, 1973.
269 Avicenne, *De l'ame humaine*, tr. A. M. Goichon, Paris, 1951.

270 "Mohammedanism" is the late nineteenth century term that was often used for Islam. Steiner—and others—also frequently spoke of the "Turks," with which Islam is meant.
271 The "Christ impulse" is the particular term Steiner used to indicate the death on the cross and the resurrection of the Son of God. This impulse is an historic *and* supersensible fact ("mystical" fact) which is operative independently of Christianity as such.
272 "Kismet" is the Turkish word for destiny, predestination.
273 See Genesis 1. The Hebrew word *Elohim* is plural while the verb *bara* (create, separate) is singular. The meaning is then something like "the unity of the Elohim created." According to Steiner, the cosmos and the human being develop themselves in creation, but so do the different categories of angels/gods. "Retarded Elohim" then means those divine beings who did not develop (further) under the influence of "ahrimanic beings." Ahriman is the evil power that impedes development. Facing him stands the evil power of Lucifer who wants to accelerate development.
274 Steiner speaks here of several Turkmen tribes that, beginning around 1050, invaded the West in ever repeating waves. The Mongols belong to these.
275 The blue God of Heaven, Tengri (see chapter 3).
276 The Archai are one of the categories in the angelology of Rudolf Steiner, which follows the teaching of Dionysius the Areopagite (mid-sixth century) and Catholic tradition in general, albeit that he gives it his own esoteric interpretation. The Archai are the Spirits of Personality; they bring the impulse of the individualization of the human being.
277 "Transubstantiation" is the Catholic view that the bread and wine actually change into the body and blood of Christ during the celebration of the Eucharist.
278 Rudolf Steiner distinguishes the sentient soul, the intellectual- or mind soul, and the consciousness soul. In the course of the history of humanity these three soul forms come to development. The consciousness soul had to awaken around 1500 AD.
279 The "higher elements" (the spirit) consist of three parts: the spirit self, life spirit and spirit man.
280 Realism and nominalism were the two principal scholastic streams in the late Middle Ages. Realism is based on Plato and the world of ideas—which is real. Nominalism is based on Aristotle who said that general concepts do not refer to spiritual ideas, but we need them to arrive at knowledge.
281 "Lemurian time" is the name Rudolf Steiner gave to the epoch of earth development preceding the Atlantean period. The book of Genesis in the Bible describes this as Paradise.
282 Zarathustra proclaimed the Soashyant, the Redeemer. Steiner relates his "Zarathustra Jesus" to this Messiah figure from the Avesta.
283 Sura 19:27-33.

www.ingramcontent.com/pod-product-compliance
Lightning Source LLC
Chambersburg PA
CBHW030856170426
43193CB00009BA/630